C000260446

THE KING OF CAPPIELOW

THE KING OF CAPPIELOW

JOHN RIDDLE

Foreword by Sir Alex Ferguson CBE

APEX PUBLISHING LTD

First published in 2008 by
Apex Publishing Ltd
PO Box 7086, Clacton on Sea, Essex, CO15 5WN

www.apexpublishing.co.uk

Copyright © 2008 by John Riddle
The author has asserted his moral rights

British Library Cataloguing-in-Publication Data
A catalogue record for this book
is available from the British Library

ISBN   1-906358-21-4   978-1-906358-21-1

All rights reserved. This book is sold subject to the condition, that no part of this book is to be reproduced, in any shape or form. Or by way of trade, stored in a retrieval system or transmitted in any form or by any means, electronic, mechanical, photocopying, recording, be lent, re-sold, hired out or otherwise circulated in any form of binding or cover other than that in which it is published and without a similar condition, including this condition being imposed on the subsequent purchaser, without prior permission of the copyright holder.

Typeset in 12pt Times New Roman

Production Manager: Chris Cowlin

Cover Design: Siobhan Smith

Printed and bound in Great Britain
By Biddles Ltd., Kings Lynn

I would like to dedicate this book to two people who have in recent years departed this mortal coil.

My mother Lena who died in 2005.
She was the inspiration behind everything I did in my life. She supported and encouraged me when others gave up. I miss her companionship and wicked sense of humour.

and

Alexander Mitchell Blake, my partner Lorna's dear father.
He lived in Albert Road, Gourock, next door to The Spinnaker Hotel, and encouraged me in most things I did.
To me he was always 'The Monarch of the Glen'.
After his funeral in Greenock, Alistair, as he was better known, was laid to rest in his beloved Tarbert, Loch Fyne, in July 2007.

May they both rest in peace.

Acknowledgements

I would like to thank the following people for their assistance and guidance in writing *The King of Cappielow*.

Ronnie MacKay - sports writer - *Scottish Sun*.
Elizabeth Ritchie - Andy's mum.
Chris Anderson - Greenock Morton fan.
Alan Hay - Greenock Morton fan.
Graham Barnstaple - Motherwell FC.
Mark McGhee - Motherwell FC.
Jonathan Mitchell - Greenock Morton Albert Hotel Supporters Club, Gourock.
Stewart McCartney - The Spinnaker Hotel, Gourock.
Neil Brown - Statistician - www.Neil brown@newcastlefans.com.
Jim Sinclair - photographer.
Ken Richardson - *Gourock & District Magazine*.
The Family of Morton Fans.
Lorna Young (née Blake), my long-suffering partner from Gourock.
Other people too numerous to mention.

And last but by no means least:
'The King of Cappielow' - Andy Ritchie

Contents

References

Vincent P. Gillen - Greenock Morton 1874-1999 (McLean Museum & Art Gallery, 1998)

Tim Gallagher - The Independent

The Sunday Herald

The Scottish Football Writers' Association

The Celtic Fanzine

Graeme Ross - Morton Greats (Breedon Books, 2004) and More Morton Greats (Breedon Books, 2005)

Martin Tyler - Sky Sports Television

The British Broadcasting Corporation

The Curator - McLean Museum & Art Gallery

Roy Dyer - fan now living in Australia

The Daily Record

Chick Young - BBC Scotland and Dukla Pumpherston

Craig Brown - The Game of My Life (Blake Publishing, 2001)

Arthur Montford - broadcaster and lifelong Morton supporter

Jim McLean - Hamilton, Clyde, Kilmarnock and Dundee United

John Mullin - journalist and Morton fan

Ronnie Miller - policeman and Morton fan

Andrew M. Cubie - football supporter

Allan McGraw - Hibernian and Greenock Morton

Peter Livingstone - football writer

Roger Graham, sports editor, Greenock Telegraph

Benny Rooney - Morton Manager 1976-83

Mike Jackson - assistant manager, Morton, 1976-83

Ian Archer - writer and Morton fan

Statistical information, Copyright © 1998-2007 Statto Organisation Limited

Foreword

It is a pleasure to write the foreword to this book *'The King of Capplielow'*.

Andy Ritchie was the bane of my life when I was at Aberdeen. He would continually score free kicks against us. So much so that we spent a whole week training in ways to defend against his great ability to score from all sorts of different positions at free kicking.

We tried everything to stop this, we tried two players on the posts, we tried leaving a gap in the wall so that our goalkeeper could see the ball.

We tried everything but two goalkeepers which was unfortante that the rules did not allow it.

Andy had a great talent and I can vouch for that as no one suffered more against it.

In closing, I hope you enjoy this book as much as I did!

Enjoy the book!

Sir Alex Ferguson CBE

Introduction

Andy Ritchie was the first Celtic player to graduate from the Celtic Boys Club and he later became Scottish Footballer of the Year.

That may be a precis of Andy's career, but lovers of the beautiful game, who stand on the windy terraces at Cappielow Park, tell a very different story.

Andy Ritchie was born in a small town two miles north of Motherwell. He is just one of a plethora of famous sons and daughters from this North Lanarkshire town. In the world of politics Robin Cook and Dr John Reid immediately spring to mind, and from the world of entertainment Sheena Easton and the Soup Dragons.

But, of course, football was the name of the game in Bellshill and other great names from the world of soccer include Sir Matt Busby, Barry Ferguson, Craig Brown, Peter Grant, Ally McCoist, and the King of Cappielow - Andy Ritchie.

Although Andy Ritchie played for Greenock Morton from 1976 to 1983, scoring 133 goals for the club in just 246 games, he is still worshipped by the fans more than 25 years later. You can still buy the legend's shirt in the Morton Club shop today.

So where did the legend start? Where did it all go wrong? And, above all, where is Andy Ritchie today a quarter of a century after he abdicated his role as '*King of Cappielow*'?

John Riddle

The Early Years

Andy Ritchie was born on 23rd February 1956 in Bellshill, a town of some 20,000 people. Bellshill is about two miles north of Motherwell where Andy also made eight appearances, scoring once after his glory days at Cappielow Park.

Andy's parents, Andrew and Bessie - or Elizabeth, to give his mum her Sunday name - had three children, Liam, Jan and Andrew. The family lived happily in the council house at Bellshill and Bessie Ritchie still lives there today, Andy's dad having died in 1996.

Andy Ritchie is immensely proud of his family. He loves his mother, naturally, his children Mark and Stephen and his granddaughter, his little princess, Keira. He's a real family man, despite what you may have heard.

Andy was educated at Belvedere School, where the headmaster was Craig Brown, the former Scotland manager. He then moved up to the 'big school', which seems appropriate for a lad who dwarfed his contemporaries. He continued his education at Bellshill Academy, eventually leaving with three 'O' levels including the all-important one in Geography. This would serve him well in later life as he travelled around the Scottish Premier League (SPL) as a delegate, touring Europe in search of talent as a scout at Celtic, Villa and Watford and, who knows, maybe one day as a UEFA delegate.

In the evenings, and because his mates all attended the Bellshill YMCA, Andy went along with the crowd. It was whilst at the YMCA that Andy was spotted by Celtic's chief scout, John Dempsey, and he was invited to join Celtic Boys Club. Dempsey's son Jimmy also played professional football at Hamilton.

Celtic Boys Club, founded in 1966, has never been affiliated to Glasgow Celtic FC, if you believe one statement that was issued in 1996. It may not have been, but its past President was Jock Stein CBE. In the details relating to the Celtic Boys Club history, in a match between Celtic Park and Dundee St Columba on 13th May 1972, which resulted in a 2-1 win for Celtic, the players who eventually signed for SPL team Celtic are highlighted with an asterisk (*) and Under-16s players' names highlighted are the team captains: **McCluskey**, **McCafferty**, *McAleer, **O'Hara**, *Kelly, **Hughes**, **Headley**, *Lee, *Ritchie, *McKee, *Little, Sub: **McGuire**.

So Andy Ritchie is there - playing for Celtic Park in 1972 - and he was the first player to graduate to Celtic FC.

In *Scottish Football Today* in 1990, in an article by Charles Stewart on The Celtic Boys Club, which was written at a time when Aberdeen and Dundee United were on the lips of all young Scottish fans.

The 'New Firms' as opposed to the 'Old Firms' were putting in place youth schemes to develop and produce more home-grown talent. This was to stop the drain of good Scottish talent south to England.

Celtic Boys Club from the East End of Glasgow can claim to have produced many quality players of outstanding skill who later would pull on the famous hooped jersey of Celtic. In fact the Celtic side that beat Dundee United in the semi-final of the Skol Cup contained five Celtic Boys Club players, all Scotland internationals: Paul McStay, Peter Grant, Derek Whyte, Steve Fulton and Gerry Creaney.

Those that were thought to have slipped through Celtic's fingers included Joe Miller, John Collins, Alan Brazil, Pat Nevin and Tom Boyd. The reasons for the slippage may be explained much later.

Jock Stein, manager of Celtic FC at that time, took an interest in Celtic Boys Club and decided that the boys should be given full access to the facilities at Barrowfield, and the then chief scout, John Higgins, suggested that the link should be forged and strengthened. He wanted the boys club to operate an Under-16 team, as he hoped that by catching the lads at an impressionable age they could be coached in the 'Celtic way' and eventually play for the Parkhead team. John Higgins had been a member of the double winning side at Celtic in the early 1950s when Jock captained the team, and he is credited with the signing of the five lads -Kenny Dalglish, Danny McGrain, David Hay, Lou Macari and George Connelly - who later were dubbed 'The Quality Street Kids'.

The future success of the club seemed assured in 1970 when Frank Cairney was appointed to the position of General Manager. Frank was on his way to Hamilton Academicals as Assistant Manager, but was persuaded to take on the Boys Club's Under-16 side.

The Celtic Boys Club produced a plethora of talent, such as Charlie Nicholas, Paul McStay, Tommy Burns, George McCluskey, Roy Aitken and Jim McInally, formerly manager of Morton. The Celtic Boys Club roll of honour is impressive, and it became even more so when Andy Ritchie came through the ranks.

"The constitution of the club makes interesting reading:

"The Club shall be known as 'The Celtic Boys Club'.

"Its objective are to provide a safe environment for children aged between 6 years and 19 years; to organise social, recreational and sporting events for its members and improve the conditions of life for its members.

"Membership of the Club will be open to all persons, regardless of nationality, political or religious beliefs, race or sexual orientation, who accept the aims of the club and reside in Glasgow and its environs.

"On the subject of leadership, the Boys Club have laid down procedures and each leader will have to go through the current approved vetting system in place at Disclosure Scotland.

"Leaders will abide by the club rules to ensure a safe environment for players under their control.

"Great lengths have been taken to ensure that everyone reading this book will know the background to Celtic Boys Club and their 'relationship' with Celtic FC."

In addition to providing a safe environment in which boys could play football locally, the Celtic Boys Club did undertake tours abroad. On one famous trip to America, the club attracted the attention of the local police, although reports are very sketchy as to why the police became interested in a touring football team. However, nothing was to come of the police involvement and Celtic Boys Club's reputation remained intact.

The founders of the Celtic Boys club 40 years ago can now look back with pride at what they have achieved.

Commitment, endeavour and dedication have kept Celtic at the top of Scottish Football and the future of Celtic Boys Club is assured. The Celtic family are known worldwide.

Morton fans are especially grateful to the Celtic Boys Club. It was from their ranks that Andy Ritchie came and later assumed the mantle of 'The King of Cappielow'.

It is accurate to say that Craig Brown had an influence on Andy's early years and he was the first man to spot his potential.

Craig Brown was an educated player in the true sense of the word. He was a schoolteacher and later, Andy recalls, he became a headmaster. Brown played at the top, winning a League Championship medal with Dundee before in later life becoming manager of the national team. He is currently working as Director of Football at Derby County in the English Premier League.

As a teenager Andy began to attract the attention of football scouts from both north and south of the border. He had trials at Manchester United, at the time under the management of Sir Matt Busby who was also born in the Bellshill area. Andy recalls going down to Old Trafford with his mother and father for a trial. United invited him back but he had his heart set on staying in Glasgow. He also went to Coventry City, Everton and Middlesbrough as well as Rangers and Celtic.

Allegedly, at the height of Andy's career, Manchester United put in a bid for Andy, but of course he was never told about that until many years later.

In those days there were regular exhibition or trial matches, and at one such game Stan Anderson, the Middlesbrough manager, and his assistant Harold Shepherdson (who had also been assistant to Sir Alf Ramsay in the 1966 World Cup) attended along with scouts from Manchester United, Coventry, Everton and the Old Firm.

Anderson and Harold where so impressed with young Andy that he was twice invited to Ayresome Park, including a period one Christmas.

Many years later, a player that Andy helped to restart his career would sign for Middlesbrough from Albion Rovers. Andy was player/manager at Rovers and suggested to Bernie Slaven that if he did well at the club he would assist him in getting a move to a big club. Bernie did do well and was awarded Player of the Year for the Division. Subsequently Middlesbrough snapped him up for £25,000, and he became a legend at the old Ayresome Park Ground, which had once been home to Brian Clough, Wilf Mannion and other greats of their day.

On one trip to Las Palmas with the Scottish Professional Youth Squad, Andy recalls: "Rangers asked me to sign and so did Middlesbrough. Manchester United had me down at Old Trafford and wanted me to go back. It was when I came back from United that Celtic stepped in. I have always been a Parkhead fan and jumped at the chance of signing."

His heart was in Glasgow and Scotland.

On Thursday nights he would train with Rangers and on Tuesdays at Celtic. I am not sure whether at the time either of the giants knew of Andy's involvement with the other club.

In the end, Andy decided that perhaps he was too young to travel to England, which was a tad too far from his family, and so he opted for Celtic and signed for them in 1971, primarily due to the youth team coach Wally Fernie. "I really liked Wally. He was a great guy," Andy told me in one of our many meetings.

Andy didn't make an immediate impact at Celtic and he was 'farmed out' on one occasion to a club in New Zealand,

Guisburn City. This was a real shock for a lad who had been reluctant to move to England, never mind to the other side of the world. Andy recalls that the standard of play in New Zealand at the time was dreadful. "Some of their players couldn't trap a medicine ball," he laughed.

Contact was made with City and the local newspaper about the big fella's stay down under, but at time of going to print no response has been forthcoming.

It's fair to say that at our first meeting Andy and I were complete strangers, but I was beginning to warm to this guy and I like to think that we later became good friends.

Rob Roy
Two Cups and a
Packet of Goals!

Andy was soon back in bonnie Scotland at Celtic, but the Glasgow giants farmed him out again, this time to a junior team, Kirkintilloch Rob Roy, a little nearer his home in Bellshill.

Rob Roy was founded in 1878 and so is much older than many of the Football League clubs. A group of young men from the Eastside of Kirkintilloch formed the club using the then defunct name of a Perthshire Curling Club. That was quite appropriate, as years later Andy became a master of curling, curling the ball that is around the oppositions wall.

At first the club only played friendly matches, but in 1927 they joined the Scottish Junior League. However, some 40 years later, in 1968, Junior Football was reorganised on a regional basis and Rob Roy joined the Central Region of the Scottish FA.

The club have moved grounds several times. In the early 1900s they settled at Kelvindale Park, which was to be their home for more than 30 years. In 1936 they relocated again to their present home, Adamslie Park, which prior to that had been the home of another junior club, Kirkintilloch Harp.

So, although Andy Ritchie had been farmed out from one of the most famous clubs in Scotland, he had gone to another club, albeit non-League, that had a proud and long history. The 1961-62 season was their finest. Kirkintilloch Rob Roy, known to all simply as Rob Roy, won the Scottish Junior Cup, the Central League Championship, the Coronation Cup and the Dumbartonshire Cup.

Rob Roy's place in Scottish non-League history was assured.

It was whilst at Rob Roy that Andy Ritchie began to attract rave notices from the media. Prior to the move, he'd had some success at Celtic Boys Club too, having rattled in an incredible 110 goals in one season.

An old relation of Andy's, who has sadly passed away, kept many press cuttings from that era, which hadn't seen light of day for more than 25 years, the pages yellowed with age. The Ritchie family archivist, Andy's son Mark, who is Morton through and through, shared the contents of the many scrapbooks with me and so I have included many references to those early days.

On 4th October 1972 the *Kirkintilloch Herald* reports on the game between Wishaw and Rob Roy: "Two second half goals from big Andy Ritchie give no measure of Rob Roy's superiority over their hosts at Recreation Park. Wishaw were outclassed and must think themselves lucky to get away with a two goal defeat by this very competent and fluid Rob Roy side. Although Ritchie gets the glory this was a first class team performance which caught the eye. Wishaw 0 - Rob Roy 2."

A week later, on 11th October, Andy was at it again. Under the local press report headline "Goal happy Rabs win through" it reads: "Rob Roy took on the might of experienced Perthshire and although slow to assert their strength turned on a blazing performance to win." Andy's contribution was a hat-trick, with Watchman and Murphy adding one each in the 5-0 win.

In December 1972 Alan Davidson, writing in the *Evening Times*, spots the raw talent of Andy Ritchie that was to grace the grass at Cappielow Park for seven glorious years. I don't need to tell you chapter and verse about the game with Blantyre Celtic, as the report's headline says it all: "Ritchie Rabs' danger man".

The rave reviews continued after the game.

That widely circulated publication, the *Kirkintilloch and Bishopbrigg Herald*, gives a fuller account of the 1-0 win over Celtic: "Rob Roy took another step towards retaining the Sectional League Cup on Saturday with a first half goal from Andy Ritchie clinching the game." It was a game of many misses and the *Herald* goes on to add: "Ritchie looking goal hungry tested the keeper soon after with an overhead shot and finally got the goal he deserved." In the 28th minute he latched on to a through ball and Thomson (the Celtic keeper) hardly saw the ball as the striker smashed it past him. The report concludes by saying: "Blantyre Celtic's goal must have had a charmed life. It must have if Ritchie only scored once instead of his usual double."

But Andy's scoring days at Rob Roy were numbered. In effect, he became a victim of his own success.

A press report from the family archives, although from what publication it's impossible to say due to the yellowing, reads: "The goal scoring days of golden boy centre forward Andy Ritchie, 33 goals in 21 games, with Rob Roy are numbered. As a result of 'Rabs' defeat by Cambuslang Rangers in the third round of the junior cup, the 16 year old Celtic provisional has been given his Parkhead call up date."

The date is 10th February, after hotshot Andy plays for 'Rabs' in the final of the Sectional League Cup against Benburb at Shawfield. Celtic wanted 6' foot 2" Ritchie immediately, but agreed to wait until after the cup final.

On 13th January 1973 the *Evening Times* has a small article on Andy's return to Celtic in which Alan Davidson writes, under the banner headline: "33 Goal Andy for Parkhead". "Celtic are calling up teenage striker Andy Ritchie who has been with Rob Roy from the start of the season. The tall, powerful 16 year old will move to Parkhead after the Junior Cup Final."

Celtic assistant boss, Sean Fallon, asked for Ritchie after Rob Roy went out of the Scottish Cup but agreed to let him stay until after the SL Cup final.

Andy's manager at the 'Rabs', Davie Brown, commented: "I

am sure that Andy has a great future in the game. He is a natural goal scorer, gets them from any distance with both feet and his head. We'll certainly be very sorry to see him go but we knew he wouldn't be with us too long after we saw his performance."

That turned out, as Morton fans know, to be a most prophetic statement from the Rob Roy manager.

At Rob Roy the goals kept coming and Celtic recalled their rough diamond.

It was against such a background that Andy said goodbye to his teammates in Kirkintilloch and returned to Parkhead.

The Pride of Parkhead

In February 1973 Andy made his debut for Celtic Reserves, scoring in the 5-0 win over Motherwell, but his return to Celtic was not a happy time. He saw things at the club that turned his stomach, but was unable to talk about them until almost 30 years later. There were obviously good times, too, as were recorded in the media at the time.

It was whilst at Celtic that Andy was called up to the Scottish Youth International Squad and on one occasion he went to Paris with the team, which included the legendary Willie Miller. Miller won many honours in the game, including being inducted into Scotland's Hall of Fame. Willie and Andy would face each other many years later in a Bell's League Cup semi-final at Hampden Park. Willie Miller remains very much involved at Aberdeen Football club today and The Dons are involved in European Cup action again this season.

In an aged press cutting, dated September 1973, Andy was in the Celtic party set to play in the European Cup in Finland against their top side at the time, Turun. Although Andy was not included in the pool of players, Celtic boss Jock Stein is quoted as saying that Andy was present with the team to pick up valuable European experience. Jock described Andy as one of the promising youngsters on the League Champions' books. However, their relationship was to sour over the next three years.

The 17-year-old Andy was now commanding a regular place in the reserves and toured Iceland and Italy with The Hoops, and in December 1973 Andy was given his big chance by Jock Stein when he was named as sub in the forthcoming game versus Dunfermline. Stein said at the time that the move was not permanent but was to give Andy experience. "At the moment he is doing well in the reserves so he deserves his chance," said Jock.

So he was given his debut against Dunfermline and, as Celtic led 4-0, there was little pressure on Andy, but it is a matter of record that 'the lad done us proud'.

Andy was described in the press at the time as a big, physical lad who was seen as a playmaker with a terrific shot. They were not wrong! Andy was the type of player that Celtic were always on the look out for and their fans enjoyed watching.

The family kept one of his Celtic payslips from that time. Andy Ritchie's take-home pay was just £37.28p. Compare that with the wages today!

All things considered, Andy went into 1974 in good heart, and he continued to hit the headlines for Celtic with his goalscoring prowess. He was knocking on the first team door.

Once commentator writes: "Andy Ritchie's baptism of fire at Dunfermline didn't seem to affect him at all. He is a big, strong, physical player who is both a playmaker and packs a hell of a shot."

Another reporter writes, under the headline "Andy stars in his new role", "The reserve team got back into action with a 4-1 win over Aberdeen. The prompting of Jimmy Johnstone and George Connelly kept the younger players on their toes."

Jimmy was revered by Andy Ritchie as possibly one of the greatest players he shared a pitch with.

The report of the game went on. "Andy Lynch put Celtic ahead but The Dons equalised and we went in level at half time."

After the break Celtic went ahead with goals from Bobby Lennox (2) and Dixie Deans.

The report concludes with this assessment of Andy Ritchie's performance: "Young Andy Ritchie keeps up his improvement. The switch from centre to midfield has proved a winning stroke. Some of his through passes in the second half had the stamp of real soccer class."

Later in the year another report reads: "Young Andy is four goal ace." In that article it describes how it would be a week for Andy to remember. In the event, Andy Ritchie had many weeks like that. This referred to a match against Hamilton Academicals Reserves in April in which he slotted home four goals in a 5-2 win.

The report concluded, "The boy is confident and has an abundance of ability." There would be few fans at Morton who would disagree!

As well as playing in the reserves, Andy was also a member of the youth team squad at Celtic and went on tour with them to Holland. They took part in a ten-team international tournament, the first game being against Dutch giants Ajax. The young Celtic player's performances were noted as the Hoops beat Ajax 2-1, followed by a win over HVB by the same score. They then thrashed Antwerp 3-0 and held the Fulham side to a goalless draw.

George McCluskey scored for Celtic against Antwerp and, along with Ritchie, who was identified as one of the stars of the competition, they now faced local club Haarlem in the final. Unfortunately, they lost 1-0 before a crowd of 8,000, but it should be noted that in the second half the Celtic boys hit the woodwork on three occasions.

Also in 1974, as the Scotland World Cup squad were preparing to do battle in West Germany, Andy Ritchie was making his own plans to be there. No sooner had he come back from Holland than he was planning his trip to Germany to watch Scotland play against the brilliant Brazilians, including Andy's hero, Roberto Rivelino.

So Andy packed up his car and, together with a pal, drove across Europe to a little village called Smitten. They got digs there and were able to watch the Scotland team train. This team included Celtic stars Danny McGrain, the legendary Jimmy Johnstone, Kenny Dalglish, David Hay and former Morton legend Joe Jordan, who by that time was at Leeds United.

Imagine Jordan and Ritchie in the same team!

In the match against the South American all-stars, Scotland drew 0-0, and then drew 1-1 in their match against Yugoslavia.

The win over Zaire was not enough, and Brazil and Yugoslavia went through to the knockout stage. Scotland were eliminated by virtue of the one goal they conceded against Yugoslavia and the Scotland squad flew back to Glasgow unbeaten but out. However, Andy stayed to watch Rivelino train every day, bending the ball round a cardboard wall.

Brazil would finish in a disappointing fourth place, unlike the previous World Cup when they beat Uruguay in the semi-final thanks to a Rivelino rocket. In the final in 1970 Brazil would meet the cream of Europe, the Italians. As one commentator said at the time: "Yes, the Italians were like cream - rich and thick." How unkind! There was no contest. The 1970 World Cup went to Brazil, who won 4-1. They of course had won the trophy three times and FIFA decided the Samba Boys would keep the trophy forever.

When the 1974 World Cup was over, with Germany beating Holland 2-1 in the final at Munich, our hero, Andy Ritchie, returned home to Glasgow, his head full of thoughts about how he would practise every day and try to emulate his hero from South America, Roberto Rivelino. The impact Rivelino made on Andy Ritchie would manifest itself in later years as, contrary to popular belief, the big Scot practised hours on end trying to 'bend it like Rivelino' long before the days of Beckham.

Andy hadn't expected to be picked for Scotland at that time, but who was to say that in 1978 the big Celtic striker would not be leading the Tartan Army in Argentina? One man would influence that dream - Jock Stein.

Andy hoped he would be able to show the South Americans a thing or too when he made the trip to Argentina as part of the Scotland team. If nothing else, Andy had an air of confidence in abundance. That may well have been his undoing. In the event, Scotland did qualify in 1978, but Andy did not make his dream trip to South America.

Scotland again would not get past the first group stages. In the opening game they lost 3-1 to Peru and then could only draw with group whipping boys Iran. It was Iran's only point of the tournament but it cost Scotland dearly. In the final match against Holland the team pulled out all the stops and recorded a famous 3-2 win over the Dutchmen, but Holland qualified on the same points as Scotland and, due to that one goal conceded to Iran, the Dutch team went through on superior goal difference.

Holland topped the next group stages ahead of West Germany and Italy to meet hosts Argentina in the final. Argentina would win 3-1 thanks to two splendid goals from Kempes and one from Bertoni. Nanninga would get Holland's consolation.

Andy would be still be only 26 years old by the time the World Cup roadshow arrived in Spain for the 1982 finals, by which time he had more Premier League games under his belt and a First Division title, and the cries of "Ritchie for Scotland" were heard regularly around Cappielow.

But would he be in Spain? And, more important for the travelling Tartan Army, would Scotland qualify again?

In 1975 Celtic aimed to win back their title, and Jock Stein included Andy Ritchie in the first team squad. In addition to Andy, the team photograph for August of that year shows Jackie McNamara, Kenny Dalglish, Peter Latchford, Dixie Deans, Danny McGrain, Bobby Lennox and George Connolly. Yes, our hero was included in the first team photograph aged just 19 years.

Also in 1975 Andy Ritchie had another "match of his life", as it was described at the time.

On Friday 7th November Andy and Rena were married at St Columba's Church, View Park, Uddingston, the town that boasted being the birthplace of the legendary Jimmy 'Jinky' Johnstone. Andy's best man was brother Liam, and Rena was attended by bridesmaids Jan, Andy's sister, Mary, Rena's sister, and a cousin, Tricia. The lavish reception was held at the Castle Rooms in Uddingston.

Yes, the 'king' was in the castle long before he was 'king'.

The day after the wedding, Andy travelled with the team to play away at St Johnstone Reserves.

Reports indicate he scored on one of the days!

On the team coach it was apparently a tradition for the newly-wed player to sing his favourite song and in return the lads on the bus would have a whip-round. Andy, true to his word, sang on the coach's PA system, much to the amusement of his teammates. He couldn't really sing, but bashed out a fair impression of 'Ole Blue Eyes' singing 'I Did It My Way'.

It was probably that outlook on life that angered Jock Stein - Andy doing it his way, not his awful singing.

Anyway, the resulting whip-round of more than £300 was enough to buy a three-piece suite for Andy and Rena's new home. The union with the lovely Rena would produce two fine sons: Mark, born in 1978 at St Francis Nursing Home in Glasgow; and Stephen, born in 1980 at Stobhill Hospital also in the city. In true Ritchie tradition, Stephen supports Celtic and Mark is Morton through and through.

On 11th February 1976 Andy played in a challenge match versus the mighty Leeds United. Needless to say, Andy scored! The big clubs in England were beginning to take notice.

In March Andy was struck down with influenza for a second time and missed out on several opportunities to impress Big Jock, but he did not go unnoticed when he was around Jock.

On one famous occasion Andy recalls being told by Stein, "If you take the cotton wool out of your ears and put it in your mouth, you may be a better player."

Their relationship did not improve with age.

Some pundits have told the tale of how Andy ignored Jock's instructions from the dugout. He placed the ball for a free kick, with his mentor screaming from the touchline, and smashed it into the net. It is alleged that Andy then turned to the bench and gave Jock the two-fingered salute.

"That's not what happened at all," insists Andy. "Yes, I did hear his instructions and went ahead and scored anyway. But I would never have dared gesture in that way. As I remember it, I smiled and waved to him - using my full hand, not two digits," he added.

There is a picture at the time of the handsome young man sitting on the bonnet of what looks like a Ford Consul with the caption: "Looking forward to the Old Firm clash … Celtic's Andy Ritchie, the new star who could play against Rangers".

But if Andy did play in that game, his days were numbered at Parkhead.

The Glasgow press were not happy when in 1976 it was announced that Andy Ritchie had joined Morton. Rumours at the time were that he'd had one too many arguments with the legendary Celtic manager Jock Stein, which ultimately led to the young man, aged just 20 years, being transferred to Greenock Morton. In exchange for the 'thorn in his flesh' Ritchie, plus a sum of £10,000, Stein was able to bring Morton keeper, Roy Baines, to Celtic, something he had badly wanted to do, as cover for Peter Latchford.

It was probably the best piece of business that manager Hal Stewart did for the Morton club.

In the event, Roy Baines never made it at Celtic, playing only 16 times before returning to Cappielow Park where he too became a Morton great.

So Andy the 6-foot midfield striker left Celtic after five years at the club as both a junior and a professional. Although he was never given a real chance to establish himself in the first team, Andy was a big favourite with the Parkhead fans, and his departure did not meet with their approval.

There are still some Celtic fans who mourn the loss of such a great talent as Andy Ritchie. One recently wrote: "As we reflect on why such a talent spent the best years of his career plodding around the mud heaps of the Scottish League rather than gracing the San Siro or Stadium of Light in the Hoops of green and white is beyond me. Maybe Andy Ritchie was a joy to behold, but it would seem that he sold his birthright for a mess of pottage or perhaps a chicken curry too many."

Andy Ritchie was just 20 years of age when he effectively was given a free transfer to Morton. Yes, Andy Ritchie did not cost Greenock Morton a penny. But he was worth millions at today's rate.

For Andy the Celtic dream or nightmare was over, and between 1976 and 1983 he graced the pitch at Cappielow Park, where he became 'the king'. It was a move that would come back to haunt Big Jock on more than one occasions, but as always Andy would have the final word.

In the seven years that Andy was with Morton, his former colleagues at Celtic won four League championships, two Scottish Cups, a League Cup and a Youth Cup - possibly eight medals that Ritchie could have had in his trophy cabinet.

But would Andy regret his move to Morton?

Should he have followed Jock Stein's advice to put cotton wool in his mouth?

Hindsight is a wonderful mistress!

1976-77
Setting Alight the First Division

Towards the end of October 1976, Morton legend Andy Ritchie made his debut for the club being a goalless draw with Clydebank.

On 23rd February 1977, just a few months after his free transfer from Celtic, Andy was still picking up the pieces after his world of football had collapsed. It was his 21st birthday and, with his new wife of just three months, Rena, he celebrated. Rena herself was an international netball star and had reached the finals of a ladies' five-a-side soccer competition at the Kelvin Hall in Glasgow.

For now this was a honeymoon period for the couple and Andy especially seemed to be enjoying life in the First Division with Morton, netting 11 goals in 10 games for The 'Ton. He had rediscovered the scoring touch that had netted him 100 goals in a season with Celtic Boys and 33 for Rob Roy in 20-odd games.

The former Scottish Youth International acknowledged that he had been tagged lazy at his former club, but he explained that he had lost heart at Celtic. It is my belief that he'd had the heart knocked out of him.

However, it was still hoped by those that saw him play that he could make it in the top flight after his 'failure' at Celtic. And how right they were. But how many realised that making it in the SPL would mean making it with Morton?

In a press cutting that the family have dated 16th April 1977,

Andy is back on the score sheet again, netting two goals at Queen of the South before the half-time break. The game was only 11 minutes old when our hero struck the first of his two goals. From midfield Veitch sent the ball out to the right and Andy Ritchie pounced on it to crack in a banana shot that beat keeper Ball from a fully 30 yards. Andy's second goal followed a neat one-two with Goldthorpe and he slotted the ball home from close range, much to the delight of the small but select travelling band of Morton fans.

With the half-time score at 2-0, Andy trooped off for his customary fag. Yes, before going out onto the pitch he secreted a single cigarette and lighter in the toilets. Then at half-time, during the team talk, he would excuse himself and go for a few drags on the weed. It was a feature of every game he played throughout his entire career.

In *Greenock Morton 1874-1999* (McLean Museum & Art Gallery, 1998) Vincent P. Gillen quotes Peter Livingstone from a much later 1981 programme about a breath of fresh air that had arrived in Cappielow. He was, of course, referring to Benny Rooney.

New faces and a new team arrived, which gave cause for celebration. Goals came thick and fast and plenty of skills abounded with Mark McGhee in attack, Andy Ritchie in midfield right through the team to Jim Holmes at fullback.

The 1976 season was finished off with a run of 16 unbeaten games and everyone at the club was confident that promotion was possible the following season.

The Magnificent Seven
We are the Champions
1977-78

Morton set off from the starting blocks in the 1977-78 season like a cork fresh out of a champagne bottle, winning 10 and drawing one of the opening 11 games.

The first three games produced a 3-0 away win at Kilmarnock, a 4-2 win at home against Alloa Athletic and a 1-0 away win at Montrose, to give Morton a 100% start and top spot in the League.

The match that stood out for most was the 5-3 victory over Hearts in which Ritchie orchestrated the midfield play with subtle promptings and precise passes, and Mark McGhee fed off his skill to create havoc in the penalty area.

But how did Mark, now manager at Motherwell, assess the start to the season and his partnership with Andy? Was Andy as good as they say?

In an interview at Fir Park in November 2007, Mark McGhee revealed how he saw the situation over 20 years ago. He was asked how he would assess Andy's career when they played at Morton together. Mark had just been made favourite for the vacant Scotland manager's job by the bookmakers at 9/4. Alex McLeish had left to become manager of Birmingham City and recorded a win at Tottenham Hotspur in his first game in charge with a goal worthy of Andy Ritchie to seal the win.

Mark said, "Andy was as good as Glen Hoddle. Apart from one player I saw during my time at Hamburg, Wolfram

Wuttke, Andy was the best striker of the ball I have ever seen."

Newcastle were thought to be interested in signing Andy but they took Mark instead. When asked about the situation, Mark said he had no idea why that decision was made.

It should be noted that at the time Hal Stewart held the purse strings at Morton and was keen to get over £1 million for Andy, which at that time was unthinkable. His cousin Lord Westwood was the chairman at Newcastle United, so when Mark went to Tyneside for a reported £150,000, well the prospect of Stewart letting Andy go anywhere was remote.

Over the years stories circulated about a plethora of clubs coming in for Andy. However, no offers ever reached Andy's ears at the time and he remained at Morton whilst lesser players got moved to bigger clubs.

Mark McGhee played against Andy several times following his move to join the magnificent team at Aberdeen, managed in those days by Alex Ferguson, later of course to become Sir Alex. Mark recalls that every time Aberdeen faced Morton and Ritchie was in the team, Alex would be concerned as to how they could contain him.

"Andy's set pieces were legendary," explained Mark. "We tried everything we could to stop him. We tried four man walls, five man walls, split walls, staggered walls, no walls at all and any combination in between you can think of. Andy Ritchie was practically unstoppable."

Unaware that at the time the bookmakers had made Mark McGhee 9/4 favourite for the vacant Scotland job, I asked him, "Will you be going to Euro 2008 now Scotland and England have failed to qualify?"

"Oh yes, I will be there for most games," smiled Mark in reply.

But would he be there as Scotland's new manager? I wondered later.

One final question I asked Mark before I left Fir Park on that wet December afternoon in 2007 was how many of that famous Aberdeen team had gone on to become managers and how many used the 'Sir Alex method' of play.

"I didn't know there was such a method. If you mean did we learn from Alex, the answer is obviously yes. You learn something from everyone and every club you play at. It's an ongoing thing. You pick up something new almost every day - that's evolution in the game," he responded.

Mark McGhee may leave Motherwell, which will be sad for the Fir Park fans as at one stage that weekend they were second behind Celtic.

The *Sunday Express* on 9th October 1977 adds fuel to the legend that Andy Ritchie was unplayable in their report of Morton's 5-3 victory over Hearts. Although he didn't score in the eight-goal thriller, he attracted the headlines. "Ritchie puts Hearts on the Rack" read the lead.

Express reporter Gerald McNee wrote: "Call this incredible afternoon's entertainment - the Andy Ritchie Show. He was the player who had everything. He beat men at ease, sent long accurate passes which decimated the Hearts defence and was always back to help out when needed."

That was indeed a revelation, as so often Andy had been labelled lazy. However, on this occasion he was the perfect member of the team.

McNee continued. "The bare facts are that he was the architect behind four of Morton's five goals. There were of course other heroes in the Morton side - Mark McGhee scored two and was a constant thorn in Hearts' defence and John Goldthorpe showed he can still snap up chances with a well-taken double.

"Ritchie struck again with a superb corner kick which was strongly headed home by centre forward Roddy Hutchison.

"Once again Morton had fire in their belly and McGhee netted number five with a low controlled shot to put the game beyond Hearts."

It was about this time that Chick Young gave his own particular analysis of Andy's talents in a rendering entitled "Ritchie stuns Saints". Not content with Morton's 4-1 win over St Johnstone, the caustic tongue of Young once again is directed towards the Morton genius:

"Andy Ritchie's work rate falls just short of redundancy. He does not believe in sweating too heavily and sometimes he looks as though he could play football in his good suit without soiling it. But if you want to talk about style, that indefinable something, the boy just oozes it.

"Last night at Cappielow he destroyed St Johnstone with a hand in all the goals in Morton's 4-1 win which takes the Greenock side within two points of second place Hearts at the top of the First Division.

"Morton though had two games in hand and Andy Ritchie in hand. Right from the kick-off he worked his magic, rocketing home the opening goal in 20 seconds. Then George Anderson, who also had a great game, headed home a Ritchie corner. The Saints pulled one back.

"But Ritchie headed the ball down for Goldthorpe to make it 3-1 in the 54th minute and two minutes later he hit a free kick from outside of the box. What a route it took; it bent like a nine bob note. If keeper Geoghegan hadn't stopped the shot, it would have curled round the south stand and landed back at Ritchie's feet. George Anderson hit home the rebound."

Older readers will remember *Shoot* magazine, one of the first and most popular magazines on the beautiful game. Andy featured in *Shoot* in November 1977, when the magazine announced that he had stepped back to go forward. The article suggests that the move from Celtic appeared to signal a downturn in Andy's career, but he had responded in the best way possible by letting his feet do the talking.

Instead of accepting life away from the spotlight of the SPL, Ritchie set the First Division alight with his performances. The big, powerful winger earned applause at Cappielow, scoring 22 goals in his first season, and he played a key part in Morton's storming finish to the season.

However, Ritchie's performance presented a problem for the Greenock club. He was attracting attention and the question was how Morton could keep them at bay. The report inaccurately says they should receive ten times the £15,000 they paid Celtic, which of course they didn't. As stated earlier, Morton actually received £10,000 at the time Ritchie came from Celtic and Roy Baines went the other way.

Morton held on to the number one spot until 17th December 1977, when two consecutive defeats saw the team drop to 2nd place.

On 21st December 1977 a report appeared in the press labelling Andy as 'lazy'. He was also described as not being the usual schoolboy hero from the comic books and sported an unruly and tousled hairstyle. I suspect that's not the first time Andy has been labelled 'unruly' either, if his earlier run-ins with Big Jock are anything to go by.

The report goes on to describe Ritchie's frame as being more like that of a heavyweight boxer, with his shoulders slightly stooped and strolling about the pitch in a manner not unlike a man taking a dog for a walk.

The verdict from an official from another club after watching a game at Cappielow was that "The big fellow is lazy. He doesn't want to know when the game isn't going his way."

It wasn't the first time such criticism had been levelled at Andy Ritchie and it wouldn't be the last time either.

He certainly had a casual style to his play, but the wider public believed that Andy was worth anybody's admission money. "In an era where players were churned out in conveyor belt fashion with all thinking and playing the same, Andy Ritchie breaks the mould. He is a crowd pleaser, a character who has illuminated the First Division since his transfer from Celtic," commented one writer.

Andy was confronted with the 'lazy' tag on several occasions. But what the spectators and some managers did not appreciate at the time, or simply chose to ignore, was the fact that the players at Morton were part-timers. Andy, for example, would get up at 6 a.m. to hump meat about in the market at Glasgow. When he finished work at the market, a long journey over to Morton followed, which sometimes took almost two hours depending on the traffic. Andy would do his training and then travel back to his home near Motherwell.

The lad didn't train hard because very often he was knackered from the day's toil.

You could count on the fingers of one hand the number of times Andy came out of a tackle with the ball, but put the ball at his feet and he would drift past players and bewilder defenders. When Ritchie had the ball there was an air of magic and expectation. He had netted 22 goals in his first season at Morton and already had 12 to his credit this term.

Many people at the time thought that Ritchie deserved a second chance at football in the top flight, and of course he would get that second chance - with Morton.

James Findlay, writing at the time, was in no doubt about his views of Andy Ritchie: "Ritchie makes Saturday afternoons rather special. When handing out awards is one of the more pleasurable aspects of the newspaper business, he wins mine as First Division Personality of the Year. In fact he strolls it."

A New Year's Eve 2-1 win at home against Montrose and The 'Ton would finish the year in second spot. The New Year would start with a bang.

Following on from their win over Montrose, on 2nd January Morton travelled to Dumbarton and showed no signs of a Hogmanay hangover, putting four goals past the opposition, and even better was to come five days later, when the team travelled to Alloa Athletic and scored five magnificent goals without reply.

They went back to the top of the First Division.

There would be only one more match in January against Stirling Albion at home, but another 2-0 win was the response from the men of Morton.

It would be more than two months before fans at Cappielow saw their favourites again, due to the bad weather and other factors.

The team did not reappear in the League until 25th February 1978, when an away trip to Arbroath ended 2-2 and Morton dropped to 3rd place. Had the Cappielow bubble burst?

On 28th February the lads were on the road again at Airdrie and a hard-fought 3-2 win momentarily restored them to pole position.

The next few months would be a roller-coaster ride, with both Hearts and Dundee vying for the number one spot.

On 4th March Morton were at home to Kilmarnock and, although the team won 2-0, they dropped to 2nd place.

That set up a top-of-the-table clash with Hearts at Cappielow before one of the biggest crowds of the season. Morton lost 1-0 and questions were being asked again. Had Morton blown it?

On the road again and Morton picked up two points at Queen of the South with a narrow 3-2 win and then another in a dour draw with Hamilton.

Those results dropped The Ton down to 3rd spot, and this was a position they would occupy until 15th April 1978.

Earlier, however, on the 1st April 1978, Andy received some alarming news from a specialist, which he did not share with the fans immediately. X-rays had revealed a crack in a bone at the base of his spine and he was told that if he carried on playing and didn't rest his back for between three and ten weeks he could end up in a wheelchair for the rest of his life and out of the game for good.

That shook Andy! He decided not to play until he got the all clear, or that's what he initially told the specialist, but he later changed his mind:

"I got the injury in the first minute at Queen of the South and I needed a support plaster as the pain was so acute. The pain disappeared as quickly as it came and I took the support plaster from round my middle, which I suppose was to prevent me from bending. It felt okay so I decided to do some light training. I had no reaction and I told Benny to count me in.

"I had been working all season to get Morton into the SPL. I wasn't going to sit and watch from the bench. Hearts and Dundee could also go up and I don't think I could stomach that.

"I made my decision knowing the risks of permanent back damage because to me getting Morton into the Premier League was all that I could think about."

Fortunately he got the green light from the medical people to continue playing.

It was against such a background that Andy Ritchie was idolised at Cappielow.

The team didn't do much better at home to Queen of the South, but when St Johnstone visited a 4-1 would kick-start their season again.

In a satisfactory away trip to promotion rivals Dundee, Morton came away with a valuable point in a 1-1 draw. And when Morton ran in five past bottom club East Fife on 12th April, that started a five-match winning streak.

Hamilton were put to the sword 3-0 at home on 15th April and a narrow 1-0 result away to St Johnstone was followed by an equally nail-biting encounter at Stirling Albion where Morton won 2-1. Those three games over the Easter period in the five-match run put Morton back at the top of the table with just two games to go, both at home.

On 26th April Airdrie were the visitors. Airdrie had avoided defeat on nine occasions as they consolidated their mid-table position, so it wasn't going to be a pushover. But the Morton lads had the winning line in sight. That was the night that Morton won promotion to the Scottish Premier League and the town was painted blue!

The final game at home was against Dundee, who were to finish in 3rd place, despite winning at Cappielow 3-2.

Morton had 58 points, the same as runners-up Hearts, but had a superior goal difference of +43 as opposed to Hearts' +35.

Morton had pulled off a remarkable achievement: 12 magnificent home wins, 13 superb away wins, eight creditable draws and only one away defeat all season.

No doubt many of you will have your own special memories of the day Greenock Morton Football Club were promoted to the Scottish Premier League.

After the summer recess, Greenock Morton Football Club would entertain the 'Old Firm' of Rangers and Celtic and the 'New Firm' from Aberdeen and Dundee United.

Would they be able to consolidate their League position and

send the big boys away from Cappielow with a bloody nose?

The fans pondered that question during the summer months whilst Andy and the boys relaxed in the Spanish sunshine.

It was a great time to be a Morton supporter!

The Magnificent Seven 1978-79 Consolidation in the Premier League

The Anglo Scottish Cup started Morton's season in the top flight. In the opening rounds, played in August 1978, Morton knocked out Raith Rovers on aggregate 6-2, Andy Ritchie making his usual contribution.

In the second round they played host to Oldham Athletic and at Cappielow sent the English packing with a comprehensive 3-0 victory. However, the return leg at Boundary Park saw Morton go out, losing 4-0. There was no disgrace in this defeat, as Oldham Athletic went on to reach the final. Oldham were also at the time playing in the Second Division of English football. In the same season that they beat Morton 4-3 on aggregate, they also had other notable wins. They beat Sunderland 3-0, north-east neighbours Newcastle United 1-0 and also Chelsea and Fulham. So, in retrospect, the Morton result was quite creditable.

Morton had quite a good run in the League Cup, starting with a second round first leg away at Hearts. Ritchie, Scott and McNeil scored in the 3-1 win. The return leg at home saw Morton go one better, beating the Edinburgh outfit 4-1 to go through on aggregate 7-2. Andy Ritchie scored in both legs, although he was probably outshone at home by two Russell specials.

In the third round at Kilmarnock in October things went

horribly wrong, with Morton going down 2-0. However, a week later, before a crowd of almost 6,000 at Cappielow, the magnificent men of Morton turned it round with a 5-2 win, with Scott (2) Thomson, Orr and, of course, Andy Ritchie scoring the goals.

That set up a quarter-final with Hibs in November. The teams had drawn 1-1 earlier in the season and indeed three of the four games would end in draws.

At Cappielow Morton won 1-0 with a Thomson goal, but at home before a crowd of more than 8,000 Hibernian won 2-0. Morton's interest in the League Cup was over for another year.

Morton kicked off the season with a home game against Celtic, who would go on to be champions. Andy scored, but goals from Glavin and McDonald gave The Hoops a 2-1 win.

Things didn't get much better the following week when the team travelled north to Aberdeen. A Harper hat-trick was enough for The Dons to secure victory. Ritchie scored his customary goal in the 3-1 defeat.

On 26th August Ritchie scored again at Cappielow, but the defence had obviously not adjusted to life in the top flight and St Mirren scored three times to secure a 3-1 win over Morton.

On 9th September Morton finally recorded a win in the League, and an away win at that. Rooney and Russell scored in the 2-1 win at Dundee and The Tons' season was up and running at last.

The following week Morton were away again, this time in Edinburgh to face Hearts. Thomson scored for Morton in the 1-1 draw against a Hearts side that would be relegated at the end of the season along with Motherwell.

On Saturday 23rd September Cappielow welcomed Rangers. Ritchie was back on the mark with a goal, supported by another from Scott. Parlane and Johnstone scored for Rangers in the exciting 2-2 draw before are crowd of 15,053.

Morton stretched their unbeaten run the following week with a 1-1 draw at Hibs and then beat Partick Thistle at home 1-0.

However, the wheels seemed to have come off the Morton bandwagon when a Pettigrew goal just after the stroke of half-time gave visitors to Cappielow Park, Motherwell, a 1-0 lead. Ritchie scored from the spot to even it up in the 52nd minute but, as so often happens, the referee evened things up by awarding a dubious spot kick to the visitors. That was converted by Lindsay and the unbeaten run came to an end, sadly before the home fans.

The next week Morton travelled to Parkhead to face Celtic and, as so often happened in those days, the mighty men of Morton picked themselves up and gave as good as they got, coming home with a very creditable 0-0 result.

Ritchie was back to his best and scored the opening goal in the next game against Aberdeen. Teammate Russell added another to cancel out Jarvie's strike for the visitors and Morton held on to beat Aberdeen 2-1.

On 10th November 1978, however, the old chestnut of Ritchie being lazy once again raised its ugly head in an account written by Sandie Beveridge in the *Daily Record*.

In the interview Andy admitted that he was not a runner and never would be. But when he turned on his particular brand of soccer magic he became Cappielow's 'Idle Idol'.

Sandie commented: "When you listen to his footballing philosophising it's easy to understand the way he plays."

Andy told the reporter: "It's meant to be a team game isn't it? So what's the point of having eleven guys running all over the place or eleven skilful players? I think of myself as a skilful player and the whole point is to blend. I look like a lazy player on the pitch but it's taken until now for me to realise I am stuck with that style. I couldn't change it if I wanted to. So I don't worry about it. Besides I don't think I am slow. In the sprint stuff I am in the leading group and it's only when it comes to the long stuff that I am near the back. What's the point of running round and round on an ash track? I don't play on ash on a Saturday."

Andy's footballing philosophy overlapped his personal life. His wife Rena confirmed that he was idle around the house and he conceded that he didn't help his wife at home apart from washing the odd dish or two, but hastily added, "But that's not my job. I wouldn't ask Rena to sell lottery tickets."

At the time, Andy was the chief sales agent for the Morton lottery and he recalls adverts running every week inviting the public to "Give Andy a Hand". He would call in to see shopkeepers and other business people to make arrangements for them to become agents. During one period he was able to hand over a £1,000 cheque each to three local people.

Andy Ritchie's main contribution was on the field. He had already given football fans some memorable moments and was tagged as one of the few genuine characters in Scottish football at the time.

As always, some stories have a nasty habit of coming back to haunt you, and Sandie Beveridge didn't have to wait long for Andy Ritchie's response. On the next day, 11th November, when Dundee United visited Cappielow Andy found the back of the net three times in the 14th, 47th and 73rd minutes in the 3-1 win.

Ian Paul, writing in the *Glasgow Herald* on Morton's 3-1 victory over Dundee United, commented that some of Scotland's best defenders had great difficulty containing the Morton wizard, saying:

"The Morton man is a phenomenon. He wields a magical influence on all around him at Cappielow, players, bosses and fans. Only the fact that the teaspoons are unbent keeps him out of the Uri Geller league. Having seen Ritchie score three goals against United, two of them were the kind of goals that have defenders facing Mecca.

"Morton's assistant manager Mike Jackson said, 'There are some people who say he only plays 20 minutes game. But isn't 20 minutes of Ritchie better than 90 minutes of nothing?'

"Manager Benny Rooney and Jackson have wisely accepted the idiosyncrasies of Ritchie and concentrated on building the right kind of support for him. They are succeeding.

"Morton were well worth their lead which they achieved in 12 minutes, even if it came from a bizarre effort from Ritchie. He worked a clever 1-2 with Jimmy Miller and from a position inside the 18 yard line, close to the byeline, sent over what he described as a cross shot, which dipped over the head of McAlpine and into the net.

"Dundee United thought they had equalised when Hegarty found the net, only for the referee to disallow the goal for off-side. Scott intercepted a back pass and McAlpine brought him down.

"Andy Ritchie popped in the penalty with consummate ease.

"When Addison scored for Dundee United a fighting finish looked on. What we should have realised was that Ritchie was outside changing into his Superman outfit again. Sure enough 16 minutes from time he produced his pièce de résistance.

"Accepting a 'knock on' about 35 yards out he had a hasty peep at Hamish McAlpine doing the sensible by racing out of his goal. The Greenock 'Uri' then hit a perfect wedge shot all the way over the keeper into the empty goal.

"The contest was over, although the Morton crowd were very upset with referee Ian Foote when he cancelled out a fourth Ritchie goal, apparently because a teammate was off-side. The crowd recovered in time to give their hero a standing ovation as he left the field.

"Dundee keeper Hamish McAlpine left the field looking like he had been strapped to a Waltzer for 90 minutes."

Chick Young in the *Evening Times* adds his twopenn'orth on the game by adding: "Three goal Ritchie is Magic".

Ritchie scored again the following week in a 3-2 win over Hearts before the team crashed to a 3-0 defeat at Ibrox on 25th November, before a crowd of 23,547.

I must add here that fans from all over the UK responded to my appeal for information during Andy's time at Morton. Fans from Rangers, Celtic, Hearts and, of course, Morton were amongst literally dozens who sent me old press cuttings and programmes from games in which Andy featured. Sadly, however, I have been unable to make direct references to the programme contents or include the Morton Football Club crest in this tribute to Andy because of the costs involved in paying the club royalties to do so. Travelling expenditure and hotel bills alone amount to more than I will receive for writing this book. But, as Andy said more than once when referring to his life in football, "this was never about money". Still, I have been able to use photographs of fans decked in Morton shirts. One even arrived from New Jersey in the USA and another showed a Morton fan in India!

Fortunately, going back to the 25th November fixture at Ibrox, I have been given permission by Rangers to use material from the programme. It contains an article headed "Morton - today's visitors", which has this to say about Andy Ritchie:

"In attack Morton have Al Scott, Bobby Russell and of course Andy Ritchie. The Ex Celt Ritchie, a powerful 6' 1", 12 st man, has incredible touches of skill for such a big fellow and packs a ferocious shot - he has scored 15 goals for Morton this season.

"He is not the hardest worker in football and he admits he hates training … but makes up for this with his exciting play. Andy is chief sales agent for the Morton lottery."

Yes, the big fella even got Rangers to advertise the Morton lottery!

The *Daily Express* reporter wrote after the match, "For once big Andy Ritchie didn't get into the match."

Also in the programme, Benny Rooney is quoted as saying, "We like to feel we have added something to the Premier League this season."

There was little doubt that the Greenock side had brought some exciting and fresh ideas to the Premier competition. It was unfortunate that Greenock Morton were suffering like every other team in the Division because of the cut-throat nature of the championship challenge. The fine efforts of Morton hadn't quite earned them the high place they might achieve in seasons to come.

Benny Rooney added, "However, we are just happy to be in the Premier League and to be more than holding our own."

Benny, of course, was lucky enough to have a fit squad, so no fewer than six of his team had been ever present up to the Rangers clash. Andy had missed only one game and Jimmy

Rooney just two. The Morton team had a very stable look about it.

Goalkeeper and ex-Celtic man Denis Connaghan worked at the time as a representative for a soft drinks firm. Most of the team members had jobs because at Morton in those days all the players were part-timers. Davie Hayes was a joiner, Jim Holmes an engineer with Rolls Royce and Barrie Orr an apprentice engineer. Another Morton great who was ever present was Neil Orr, who was a greenkeeper at the Kilmacolm Golf Club. Jimmy Rooney in midfield was a civil servant, Jimmy Miller worked in a distillery and Bobby Thomson, who joined the club from St Johnstone and made a big impact at Cappielow, was another joiner. Also, playing up front for Morton in that fixture and returning to Ibrox for the first time since his transfer, was former Rangers striker, Ally Scott, who worked for a Glasgow building society. He had alongside him factory worker Bobby Russell and, of course, Andy Ritchie, who at that time was the chief sales agent for the Morton lottery. Add to this apprentice welder John McNeil, tax inspector Billy Hutchison and youngster Roddy Hutchinson who had scored against Hearts the previous week and you have a pen picture of the part-time team that faced mighty Rangers.

History reveals that Morton have met Rangers 96 times in the League, with the Glasgow club winning 68, Morton 12 and 15 draws. In the 1922 Scottish Cup final Morton had beaten Rangers 1-0 with a Jimmy Gourlay free kick. The team didn't immediately return to Greenock from Ibrox but instead boarded a train to play a friendly match with my hometown team, Hartlepool United. Heady days! In the 1963-64 Cup Final Rangers beat Morton 5-0 with Jim Forrest scoring four goals. Rangers had beaten Morton in the League 10-2 back in 1913, but there was not going to be a repeat of that scoreline.

Well Rangers had beaten Morton 3-0 this time, but would it be enough for them to stop Celtic?

The following week found them losing 2-1 away to Thistle, signalling to the Morton team that this was going to be a tough

Division in which to compete. Consistency had to be the name of the game.

Another away game at Motherwell saw the team draw 1-1, with Andy scoring yet another goal, this time a 55-minute penalty, only for the home team to equalise 10 minutes from time.

The next match was back at Cappielow against champions elect Celtic on the 23rd December 1978, in front of a crowd of 13,236. Celtic would clock up eight wins on the road, but this wasn't one of them. Andy Ritchie was set to give the Morton fans the early Christmas present they wanted. But like Santa Claus he kept them waiting, until the 88th minute to be precise, before slotting home a penalty past the former Morton keeper, Roy Baines, who was deputising for Peter Latchford. There was no way back for Celtic and Morton clinched an historic 1-0 win over the Glasgow giants.

The seasonal festivities continued and nobody got the sack - unless, of course, you count Santa Claus!

When Morton visited Aberdeen for the second time in that season, thoughts were obviously on the game played in August when The Dons had beaten them 3-1. But it was a very different team that visited Pittordrie this time. Had they not, since the last visit north, beaten Dundee United, who would eventually finish third in the League? Had they not the week before beaten Celtic 1-0, who would go on to win the championship by three points?

On 30th December 1978 Aberdeen were put to the sword, avenging the defeat earlier in the season. Although, goalless at half-time, Andy Ritchie scored on 60 minutes and his teammate McNeil added a second, putting the game out of the reach of The Dons. Harper did pull one back for Aberdeen two minutes from time, but it was only a consolation. Morton had held on and a happy Hogmanay was had by all in Greenock.

The League table in December 1979 makes pleasant reading for Morton fans of all ages:

Scottish Premier League, December 1979

	P	W	L	D	F	A	Pts
Morton	14	9	2	3	32	17	21
Celtic	15	9	3	3	29	14	21
St Mirren	16	6	5	5	24	27	17
Aberdeen	14	6	5	3	25	18	15
Rangers	16	6	7	3	23	22	15
Partick Thistle	16	5	6	5	19	22	15
Dundee Utd	15	5	6	4	21	17	14
Kilmarnock	15	5	6	4	16	24	14
Dundee	15	6	8	1	24	36	13
Hibernian	16	2	11	3	15	31	7

Greenock Morton would never again be the top dog in the Scottish Premier League.

It was almost three weeks before Morton figured in a League game again at home to Rangers, who eventually finished second to Celtic. Two second-half goals from MacDonald and Watson gave the visitors a 2-0 win.

The New Year had not started as the old one had finished and Morton appeared to have a hangover!

A third round Scottish Cup match against St Johnstone had been scheduled for Saturday 27th January, but it fell foul of the weather and was rescheduled for the following month. In those days it was a two-leg affair. Ritchie scored in the home leg in a 1-1 draw, but the away match at St Johnstone was a classic for Andy. He scored another hat-trick and Scott added another goal to make Morton easy winners on 4-2 and 5-3 on aggregate to set up a match with Hearts.

Back in the League, a 2-2 draw at Thistle followed by another draw away to Hibs on 24th February 1979 were not really the start Benny Rooney and his men had hoped for. But playing only four League games between 1st January and 10th March took its toll, and on the latter date worse was to come when Morton went down 4-1 to Dundee United. It was sweet revenge for United after their November drubbing at

Cappielow.

It was part of a roller-coaster season for the men from Morton as, just four days later, at Cappielow on 14th March, Morton thrashed Motherwell 6-0! Ritchie, as was often the case, opened the scoring from open play For this match, Morton welcomed home goalkeeper Roy Baines after his three-year stay at Celtic. Andy scored again at St Mirren in the next game, but it proved to be nothing more than a consolation goal. However, it did move him onto 23 League, League Cup and Scottish Cup goals for the season, making him second only to Aberdeen's Joe Harper.

The League table at the time shows Morton on the same points as Hibernian and one ahead of Celtic on 22 points.

The ups and downs continued. Andy was not on the score sheet when Dundee United were the visitors in their next game on 24th March, but The Tons ran out easy winners 3-1. Morton were in 4th spot behind the 'Old Firm'.

The *Daily Record* said at the time, "Morton won't be relegated. They have good players in Neil Orr and of course Andy Ritchie."

A trip to Parkhead was met with ruthless precision from the Celtic team and Morton lost 3-0. Originally the match had been scheduled for 3rd March but had been a victim of the weather. Andy Ritchie scored for Morton with a tremendous shot, only to have it disallowed on the intervention of the linesman's flag. Later in the game Ronnie Galvin added a third goal for the home team and Morton protested about its validity, so much so that Andy Ritchie ended up with a yellow card for dissent for kicking the ball off the centre spot.

Ritchie scored again when Hearts visited Cappielow on 31st March, but two goals from Busby and Gibson looked to have stolen the points for the visitors. Thankfully, with just five minutes to go, Thomson got the equaliser and the game ended all square.

The second home game on the trot saw Aberdeen as the visitors in what was a tightly fought encounter. Cooper scored the only goal of the game for The Dons in a disappointing result for the home fans.

An away trip back to Ibrox beckoned and Morton really did need to secure points to maintain their Premiership status. Morton took the lead after 31 minutes with a Russell goal and the visitors went in 1-0 up at half time. Morton held on to their lead until the 63rd minute when Copper equalised, resulting in a 1-1 draw.

Andy then went on a remarkable scoring spree, starting with a 1-0 win over St Mirren, when he netted the only goal in a thrilling game. His second-half penalty on 84 minutes looked to have giving Morton victory in the next game with Hibs, but on the stroke of full-time Callachan popped up to score his second of the game and give the Edinburgh outfit a share of the spoils.

Andy Ritchie was on target again, this time on the hour mark, in the 3-0 home win over Hibs on 18th April. He made it four in a row at Partick Thistle with an 88th-minute conversion. That proved to be only a consolation, with Thistle winning 2-1.

Five in a row seemed inevitable as the team went away to Motherwell. Morton were 2-0 up at half-time with a double from Thomson, but the home side rallied after the break with a brace from Irvine and one from Stevens. With just 13 minutes remaining - an unlucky 13 for Motherwell - the King of Cappielow popped up with an equaliser, scoring for his fifth game in a row.

Morton's season came to a close with a 1-0 win at Hearts and for once Andy Ritchie was not on the score sheet. A 44th-minute goal from Thomson gave Morton the points.

The result relegated Hearts along with Motherwell, and Morton retained their Premiership status in 7th place.

Morton had played and won many friends in the Anglo Scottish Cup, the FA Cup and the League Cup.

Andy had scored against Watford in a pre-season friendly, clinched a hat-trick against Meadowbank and also against Dundee United, prompting chants of "Ritchie for Scotland", and had scored against the best in the business at Celtic,

Aberdeen, St Mirren, Rangers and Motherwell. In fact throughout the season he scored a goal against almost every team in the SPL.

But Andy Ritchie hadn't finished yet.

Andy was attracting interest from many clubs in England. Manchester United, where he'd had a trial as a youngster, had him watched on several occasions. United finished the season way down in 9th position and needed a proven goalscorer. Middlesbrough, too, where Andy had spent one Christmas, wanted a striker as they hovered mid-table. Coventry, also in the top flight, had him watched and even Brian Clough at Nottingham Forest was reported to be interested.

Forest had finished runners-up to Liverpool, but whether Cloughie could have coped with Andy Ritchie is a point of debate. What is certain is that Brian Clough and Forest would go on to lift the European Cup not once but twice, in 1979 and again in 1980. A little-known Scotsman, born in Montrose, who started his career as an apprentice at Hartlepool United, would lift the top prize in Europe. His name? John McGovern.

Brighton and Leeds United were added to the list. Leeds desperately needed to replace their striking force and Ritchie seemed to fit the bill. Leeds were relegated the following season as were Middlesbrough. How they could have done with Andy Ritchie's goals. In the past several great Scottish players had plied their trade at Elland Road, including Billy Bremner, Peter Lorimer, Joe Jordan and others.

Approaches from south of the border were never revealed to Andy Ritchie and we can only speculate where this prolific goalscorer might have ended up.

But none of the offers ever came to anything and Andy was not notified until many years later when he was working as a scout in England for Watford and Aston Villa.

Morton took the team for a well-earned break to Magaluf with manager Rooney commenting at the time, "The boys deserve a break and we are having a wonderful time."

Andy and his Cappielow teammates had kept Morton in the SPL and the Greenock fans were eternally grateful.

Player of the Year Award and Scotland's Hall of Fame

In April 1979 in Glasgow the Scottish Sports Writers' Association voted Andy Ritchie Player of the Year. This was the first time such an award had been received by a player from a 'minnow'. It thrust Andy onto the international scene as well as the Scottish scene.

Andy took his dad, Andrew, and his grandfather plus an old family friend along to the presentation evening for the Player of the Year. The three men would attend many such functions over the years and several matches to boot.

His name joined many footballing greats who have won this prestigious award over the years:

1971 Martin Buchan - Aberdeen
1972 Dave Smith - Rangers
1973 George Connolly - Celtic
1974 World Cup Squad
1975 Sandy Jardine - Rangers
1976 John Grieg - Rangers
1977 Danny McGrain - Celtic
1978 Derek Johnstone - Rangers
1979 Andy Ritchie - Morton
1980 Gordon Strachan - Aberdeen
1981 Alan Rough - Partick Thistle

1982 Paul Sturrock - Dundee United
1983 Charlie Nicholas - Celtic
1984 Willie Miller - Aberdeen
1985 Hamish McAlpine - Dundee United

In the 14 years that Andy Ritchie played football in Scotland, in his time at Celtic, Greenock Morton, Motherwell and in the latter stages as player/manager at Albion Rovers, he was the only player from a 'small' club to attract the Player of the Year award.

When you look at the players who received the award and examine their playing records in detail, two questions need to be asked:

Why did Andy Ritchie only have one cap as an over-age player for Scotland?

And ...

Why has he waited more than 25 years to be inducted into Scotland's Hall of Fame?

If you look at the list of former recipients of the Scottish Football Writers' Player of the Year, at the time Andy was at his peak, the omissions are obvious.

Followers of the game will notice that below I haven't selected three lesser mortals to promote Andy Ritchie's case for inclusion in the Scottish Hall of Fame, but three giants.

Sandy Jardine, Rangers, Winner 1975
William Pullar Jardine was born in Edinburgh on New Year's Eve 1948, a date always celebrated by Scottish fans.

Jardine attracted the handle 'Sandy' throughout his career and many thought it was a shortened version of Alexander (a popular shortening of the name in Scotland). But it was actually a nickname he attracted in his youth because of the colour of his hair.

Sandy was with Rangers from 1965 and made his debut in 1967. He went on to play for the Ibrox outfit 674 times, mainly as a fullback, but occasionally as a sweeper as the game changed.

He was an integral part of the Rangers team that won the European Cup Winners' Cup in 1972, and his 13-year association with Rangers saw him capped by Scotland 38 times. He made his international debut against Portugal in 1971 and represented his country for eight years, the final time being against Belgium in 1979. Sandy played in the 1974 World Cup and again in the 1978 World Cup finals.

In the twilight of his career he moved to Hearts, whom he had supported as a boy. He worked there for six years and played 184 League games, scoring three goals to add to the 77 he scored for the Ibrox team. His association with the club continued after his playing days ended, as joint manager with another Rangers old boy, Alex McDonald.

Sandy is an inductee of the Scotland Hall of Fame.

John Grieg, Rangers, Winner 1976

John Grieg MBE played for Rangers from 1961 to 1978, clocking up more than 750 appearances and scoring a remarkable 120 goals from his position as a defender.

Born in Edinburgh, John supported Hearts as a boy but spent his entire career at Ibrox, winning three domestic trebles. He was captain of the Rangers team in 1972 when they beat Moscow Dynamo 3-2 in Barcelona. Over the 17 years he was with Rangers, in a period that some say was dominated by Celtic, John collected five Premier League titles, seven Scottish Cups, four League Cups and 44 Scottish caps.

He played for the national team from 1964 to 1971, scoring one goal in 44 starts. His crowning moment in the dark blue of his country came in the 1-0 win over Italy at Hampden Park on 9th November 1965, when he scored the late winner.

Ironically, as I am sitting penning this paragraph, Alex McLeish's Scotland team are awaiting the arrival of the Italians for the crunch match that might decide whether the national team will be going to Euro 2008.

As well as his Footballer of the Year award in 1976, the year Andy Ritchie joined Morton, John was the winner of the same award ten years earlier, in 1966.

In 1978 John entered the managerial stakes, replacing Jock Wallace after the defeat to Morton. He was not as successful a manager as he was a player and they finished no higher than second, which is not good enough for the Glasgow giants, but how many teams wish they could finish runners-up years on the trot?

In the following season in the European Cup John engineered a win over Italian giants Juventus before losing to Cologne. Two Scottish Cups and two League Cups were won in his five seasons as manager at Ibrox, but he perhaps was most credited for the signing of one player, himself to become an icon at Rangers, Ally McCoist from Sunderland.

Ally was also born in Bellshill and would play for Rangers more than 400 times in his 15 years with the club. He amassed a remarkable nine League Championship medals, a Scottish Cup and nine League Cup medals, as well attracting two nicknames, 'Super Ally' and 'The Judge', the latter during the Souness years, as he was on the bench so often.

In 1992 and 1993 he was Europe's top goalscorer and not surprisingly was voted Scotland's Player of the Year in 1992. He scored more than 251 League goals at Ibrox plus another 104 in other competitions, making him Rangers' all-time leading goalscorer.

His connection with Rangers was renewed after a spell at Kilmarnock and in 2004 he joined the Scotland national team coaching staff under his former Rangers manager Walter Smith.

Younger readers who never saw Ally play will know him from his appearances (1996-2007) as part of the *A Question of Sport* team. On his farewell appearance, chaired by Sue Barker, Ally famously failed to recognise the mystery guest … It was Walter Smith.

But the signing of this legend was not to save John Grieg and, under immense pressure from the Scottish media (always a handy scapegoat when a club wants rid) John Grieg resigned in October 1983. He went to work as a pundit for Radio Scotland and the BBC and in 2003 he joined the board at

Rangers.

John was elected to Rangers' Hall of Fame and immortalised in a statue outside Ibrox to commemorate the tragic events of 1971 at Ibrox when 66 supporters died and more than 200 were injured. The match was between Rangers and Celtic on 2nd January and was goalless until the 89th minute when Celtic took the lead. Many Rangers fans started leaving the stadium and at passageway No. 13 the barriers collapsed. This tragedy led to the redevelopment of Ibrox and it was subsequently awarded UEFA five-star status. As John Grieg was captain of Rangers at the time, it seemed appropriate to many that it should be his statue that marked the memorial.

He was awarded an MBE in 1977 and he, too, is an inductee into Scotland's Hall of Fame.

Danny McGrain, Celtic, Winner 1978

Daniel Fergus McGrain, 'Danny', was born in Glasgow in 1950. He made a total of 663 appearances for The Hoops, scoring eight goals in a career that spanned 17 years.

During that time, from his fullback position, he also won 63 caps for Scotland.

His achievements are even more remarkable when you take into account that McGrain overcame the handicaps of both diabetes, diagnosed in 1974, and a fractured skull and continued playing. He was a member of Scotland's World Cup squads of 1974 and 1982, in the latter year as captain.

As a boy Danny supported Celtic's rivals Rangers, but he went on to win League Championships with Celtic in 1979, 1981, 1982 and 1986. He was also the skipper that led Celtic to an historic win in the 100th Scottish Cup final in 1985 when they beat Dundee United.

In all, at Parkhead he won six championships, the Scottish Cup on five occasions and the League Cup twice. Also, in addition to his 62 full Scotland caps he won two at Under-23 level.

He played just 21 games for Hamilton in the 1987-88 season in the twilight of his career and had one attempt at management with Arbroath.

Danny McGrain was awarded the MBE in 1983 and he, too, is a member of the Scotland Hall of Fame.

In 1979, as we know, Andy Ritchie broke the monopoly of either Celtic or Rangers players winning the award, a run that stretched back to 1972. The press at the time and many associated with the game raised shouts of "Ritchie for Scotland", but those cries apparently fell on deaf ears.

The hat-trick against Dundee United, which was hailed as one of Ritchie's finest moments, finally convinced some at the SFA that Ritchie had to be included in the Euro-qualifying squad. Manager Jock Stein obliged his employers and Ritchie travelled with the party, expecting to play.

As we now know, Andy was offered the crumbs from the top table and named as an over-aged player in the Under-23 squad. Although he was angry, disappointed and hurt that his performance that season had not been recognised by his former manager at Celtic, now in charge of Scotland, he never once voiced his feelings. Instead he took Jock Stein's advice given to him years earlier at Celtic - he took the cotton wool out of his ears and put it in his mouth. And on this particular subject that is where it has remained for more than a quarter of a century.

Was Ritchie's relationship with the late Jock Stein to influence not only his appearances in the Scotland shirt but also his induction into Scotland's Hall of Fame?

I should say at this point that this is one chapter in the book I have not discussed with Andy Ritchie. These are my opinions based on my observations, reading the vast amount of literature that has been written about Scottish football and talking to people within the game - managers, former players and the most important people of all, the supporters of the beautiful game.

The PFA Player of the Year award began in 1978 and that too has been dominated, naturally, by Rangers and Celtic with a few odd exceptions, those notably being Mark McGhee and

Willie Miller from Aberdeen, Paul Hegarty of Dundee United, Sandy Clarke at Airdrie and Jim Duffy of Greenock Morton.

Andy Ritchie did not attract an award from his fellow professionals even though he topped the SPL scoring charts for three seasons. That would appear to say it all.

However, I did ask 'the powers that be' if they could explain the process of induction into the Hall of Fame and this is explained next.

Within the Scottish Football Museum there is a Scottish Football Hall of Fame, established in 2004. There is also an SFA International Roll of Honour, set up originally by the SFA, and predating the creation of the museum but now housed there.

The SFA International Roll of Honour is for Scottish internationals with 50 caps or more. So basically Andy Ritchie does not qualify for inclusion. There are currently about 24 individuals within the Roll of Honour, which is for the men's national team, and talks are ongoing for the introduction of a similar award for the women's national team.

The Scottish Football Hall of Fame was a long-term objective of the Scottish Football Museum. For years the SFA International Roll of Honour had been referred to as a Hall of Fame, but it obviously did not recognise great players that never received 50 caps or managers.

The Hall of Fame finally opened in 2004. There are currently 42 inductees and, at the time of writing, another nine are due to be inducted in November 2007.

Although recipients of the Footballer of the Year award, such as Andy, or players that have won more than 50 caps for Scotland do qualify as inductees into the Hall of Fame, entry therein is not automatic.

The requirements for consideration are quite simple:

* *Any Scot who has made a significant mark within football or any foreign national who has greatly enhanced the Scottish game.*

Well, if winning the Player of the Year award in 1979, the

Adidas Silver Boot, three times topping the scoring charts and attracting the comments and accolades such as 'Ritchie for Scotland' is not considered 'significant', then please pass me the *Oxford English Dictionary* as I've obviously got the meaning wrong.

* *Scottish players still actively involved in the playing side of things cannot be considered until they have stopped playing.*

Andy Ritchie retired from playing in the 1980s almost 25 years ago, although he is a SPL delegate.

* *No Scottish nationals (foreign players) can be considered until after their contribution to Scottish football has ended and their playing career has finished in Scotland.*

Andy does not qualify - if he cuts himself shaving he bleeds tartan blood.

* *The process of getting into the Hall of Fame initially involves public voting - the most popular names are put onto a short list.*

Andy Ritchie has never received enough votes to get onto the short list, so it's down to you Morton fans to register your votes, either online via the museum's website at www.scottishfootballmuseum.org.uk or by visiting the museum and voting in person.

* *The short list is presented to the Hall of Fame panel who then decide on the inductees for that particular year.*

The panel, when considering nominees for induction into the Hall of Fame, compares a wide range of merits, such as goalkeeping ability, playing skills, success on the field, leadership skills and impact within the game. It is never an easy decision for the panel.

Although 20 were inducted in the first year, that figure is likely to amount to only a handful each year. Obviously there are many players who have yet to enter the Hall of Fame, many of whom the majority might think should be considered ahead of Andy Ritchie and they are, of course, entitled to their opinion.

In the past some organisations, newspaper and supporters' clubs have started campaigns to increase the number of votes for particular candidates. The *Greenock Telegraph* ran such a campaign for Jimmy Cowan.

Jimmy started his career at St Mirren, but signed for Morton in May 1944. During his time with the club he was selected to play for Scotland 25 times, winning on every single occasion. Even when Morton were relegated he retained his goalkeeper's jersey, before moving to Sunderland and finally finishing his career at Third Lanark. The 3-1 win Scotland had over England in 1949 is often referred to as 'Cowan's Match'. He made a string of saves and was known as 'The Prince of Goalkeepers'. Sadly Jimmy died in 1968, aged just 42.

Despite the *Telegraph* campaign, Jimmy Cowan does not appear to have been inducted into the Hall of Fame, although another 'Morton' has - Alan Morton of Rangers.

Maybe when this volume hits the bookshelves it will signal a time for the *Greenock Telegraph*, the Supporters' Trust and all other Morton fans to take action to make their voices heard in respect of Andy Ritchie, 'The King of Cappielow'.

As I said at the outset, Andy has not seen this chapter relating to my thoughts about his induction into the Hall of Fame, so I hope he will forgive me for raising the issue.

As Andy once said, "I don't need trophies, medals and prizes to remind me of my time at Morton ... I have my memories."

Enough said!

The Magnificent Seven Up to 6th from Top in the Premier League! 1979-80

The 1979-80 season kicked off as it had done in the previous year with a visit to Celtic Park on 11th August. The programme on the day, priced 15p, extended a warm welcome to Morton in an article entitled "Morton blend an exciting side":

"With the experience of their initial season in the Premier Division behind them, Morton look forward to an even more successful campaign. They have given clear evidence of their intentions with decisive victories over last season's Second Division champions Berwick Rangers with an 8-1 aggregate win in the first round of the Anglo-Scottish Cup.

"Andy Ritchie's spectacular scoring exploits last season had him acclaimed by the Scottish Football Writers' Association as the Player of the Year and clearly he will produce a number of his 'specials' once again."

A second article in the programme goes on to say:

"The last time Morton visited Celtic Park on 28th March Celtic won the game 3-0. The match was originally scheduled for 3rd March but fell victim of the protracted winter shut-down. Celtic won that game 3-0. Morton protested when the third goal went in and Andy Ritchie was shown the yellow card for kicking the ball off the centre spot."

Celtic faced a tough match, as Morton had given a good

account of themselves in their first season back in the Premier Division, with a 4-0 win away at Second Division Champions Berwick Rangers and a 4-1 win at Cappielow in the Anglo Scottish Cup.

Celtic had warmed up for the first League game with a 5-0 thrashing of Clydebank in the Dryborough Cup and a 6-1 drubbing of a China X1.

Morton put up a creditable performance, going down by the odd goal in five to the champions in a close game, Celtic winning 3-2. Both of Morton's goals were scored by Andy Ritchie.

Three subsequent wins on the bounce, scoring eight goals and conceding just three against Partick, St Mirren and Aberdeen, saw Morton rise to the dizzy heights of second in the table.

There was a minor hiccup at Dundee when Morton lost by an odd goal in seven, but the team was building a reputation as entertainers, and so was the young Andy Ritchie.

But before he finally abdicated as the 'King of Cappielow' there was still work to be done.

In August Morton had a taste of international football, albeit it in the Anglo Scottish Cup.

They dispatched border side Berwick Rangers 8-1 on aggregate and then travelled to the once proud Preston North End, a club steeped in history and with their own legend, Tom Finney. Morton beat Preston 5-1 on aggregate to set up a clash with Bristol City in the semi-final. The Morton boys went down on aggregate 3-2 after holding the West Country side 2-2 at Ashton Gate.

The Anglo Scottish Cup did prove to be a popular distraction from the League and in the 1980-81 season Morton had some success again, beating Falkirk 7-3 on aggregate with Andy Ritchie scoring in both legs. They stumbled somewhat in the next round, going out to Notts County 3-1, Morton's goal being scored by - of course - Andy Ritchie.

Back in the League Morton went on a nine-match unbeaten run.

Two home wins started off the run, Morton beating Kilmarnock 3-1 to go second in the Premier League on 22nd September with goals from McLoughlin, Thomson and Ritchie. Dundee United followed and it just got better. A Ritchie hat-trick and another goal from Scott saw Morton run out easy 4-1 winners to maintain their 2nd spot.

Two away draws at Hibs and Rangers then brought Celtic to Cappielow. More than 19,600 fans crammed into the Morton ground on 20th October. A goal from Thomson, the only one of the game, gave Morton revenge for their defeat in March and saw the team maintain their runners-up spot. The fans went wild!

Morton were on fire.

Seven days later Morton travelled to Partick Thistle and, before a much smaller crowd of just over 7,000, the men of Morton turned on a stylish show. Goals from Holmes, McNeil, Thomson and our man Ritchie saw the home side blow away 4-1.

On 3rd November the fireworks anticipated in the clash with St Mirren never materialised and the game proved to be a damp squib, ending goalless. But when the Cappielow crowd went home to listen to the radio they found that other results had gone Morton's way: the men from Cappielow had taken over the number one spot in the Premier League.

Bragging rights on the Clyde belonged to Morton that week.

Aberdeen and Morton have a history of providing some first-class entertainment. When The Ton visited Pittordrie on 10th November they did not disappoint the crowd of over 11,500. Goals from Thomson and Ritchie ensured that Morton stayed in pole position and the Greenock fans could have another week with chests puffed out with pride.

The following week back at Cappielow more than 6,000 welcomed the visit of Dundee with the anticipation of another Morton win. Dundee would be relegated at the end of the season, and the reason was there for all to see as Morton destroyed the Dundee men with goals from Anderson and Ritchie from the spot.

Other results, however, meant that Morton dropped to 2nd place, a position they would then occupy until the New Year.

The weather postponed two matches and the next game was at home to Rangers, and Rangers' 1-0 win stopped perhaps what would have been the best ever run for Morton in the top flight. Apart from a 2-0 home win over Hibernian, in which Ritchie and Tolmie scored, a 3-1 defeat at Celtic on 22nd December before 25,600 and another defeat at home just before New Year's Eve meant that Morton would finish the year on a low.

Yes, Morton topped the League in December and statistics don't lie, and for a period from November to March they held on to 2nd place. During that time they beat Hibs 1-0 and Aberdeen 2-0 - and then disaster struck.

On New Year's Day 1980 Morton had a good draw at St Mirren, with Hutchison and Ritchie getting the goals. This was followed by a famous 1-0 home win over Aberdeen, McLaren getting the all-important goal.

Two subsequent defeats to Dundee and Kilmarnock were not the preparation Andy and his teammates wanted for the third round Scottish Cup tie with Cowdenbeath. However, they need not have worried as in a hard-fought game a single goal from Tolmie was enough to take them into the fourth round.

Another game was cancelled due to the weather and that was followed by a reverse at Hibernian, Morton going down by the odd goal in five.

Dunfermline were the visitors to Greenock on 16th February and Morton turned on a terrific performance, sweeping aside their visitors in a 5-0 win. Tolmie, Brown, Thomson, McLaughlin and Ritchie all found the back of Dunfermline's net, sending the near 5,000 crowd home happy.

But in the League Morton's form was inconsistent.

Following the nap against Dunfermline, Morton lost to both members of the 'Old Firm'. The trip to Ibrox resulted in a 3-1 defeat and the home tie against Celtic, although closer, gave The Hoops a 1-0 win.

Morton then met Celtic in the fifth round of the Scottish FA

Cup at Parkhead, where the home side won 2-0. Morton on the road picked up a valuable point at Kilmarnock on 12th March and then won 2-1 at home to St Mirren.

Despite their indifferent form, Morton were still 2nd from top on 15th March.

A trip north to Pittordrie proved a fruitless trip, The Dons scoring the only goal of the game and Morton dropping to 3rd place.

Two wins over Easter away to both Partick Thistle and Kilmarnock kept Morton in 3rd spot, with a chance of a European place. However, three consecutive defeats to Dundee United twice in the space of 11 days by the same 2-0 scoreline and a 1-0 home defeat to Rangers saw Andy and the boys drop to 5th with just two games to go.

A 1-1 draw at home against Hibs on 26th April and an away 0-0 draw at Dundee United saw Morton finally finish in 6th place.

It could have been so much better.

Morton had dropped two points in no fewer than nine games in the season and those 18 points would have put the team on 54 points, some six ahead of the champions Aberdeen. Speculation maybe, but Morton had beaten champions Aberdeen three times in the League and had had successes against runners-up Celtic and 3rd place St Mirren on two occasions.

Dundee and Hibernian would face the drop, but Morton had a mid-table place and were more than safe.

There were no great thrashings, but the number of times the team failed to find the net was crucial. You cannot fail to score in six out of 12 games. Morton plummeted from the top of the League to 6th, but it was still their best ever finish.

On 1st December 1979 at Hampden Park, Glasgow, Morton faced Willie Miller's Aberdeen in the semi-final of the League Cup.

Morton had beaten Queen of the South 1-0 away on 29th August with a Ritchie special. The big fella finished the job at home in the second leg, scoring twice in the 4-0 drubbing.

In the third round away to Partick Thistle on 26th September Rooney put The Ton ahead with the only goal of the match. Morton finished the job back in Greenock on 10th October with a 4-1 win, with Andy netting yet another goal.

The fourth round against Kilmarnock was a thriller. In the home leg Hutchison, Thomson and Ritchie gave Morton a 3-2 advantage, but in the return leg they lost to a single goal, which set up a penalty shoot-out. Morton won on penalties to earn their place in the semi-final against Aberdeen.

Aberdeen's route was much more convincing with aggregate wins of 5-2 over Arbroath, 7-2 over Meadowbank, 5-1 over Rangers and 4-2 over Celtic. In the early rounds Archibald scored a hat-trick, former Cappielow favourite Mark McGhee scored in three separate games and little Gordon Strachan scored three as well. The Pittordrie goal machine was on fire. Morton lost 2-1.

In the match programme, Andy once again attracted the attention of the programme writers. The front cover features Aberdeen skipper Willie Miller and Morton's captain David Hayes. It states: "Bobby Thomson, Bobby Russell, Roy Baines, Jimmy Millar and even Andy Ritchie - they all moved in with little fanfare."

In the 'star spot' feature Andy Ritchie is contrasted with the Aberdeen star Bobby Clarke, saying this about Andy:

"By the time Christmas comes around Andy Ritchie of Morton will almost certainly have hit a century of goals for the Cappielow club … in just three seasons. And those are the sort of devastating statistics Andy can throw at the critics, who insist he is a luxury of the past with no real place in modern day football.

"But there's no doubt he is one of the few controversial characters in a game which threatens to become almost monotonous in the race for efficiency. The stores about Ambling Andy are already becoming a legend.

"Like the English manager who dashed north on the strong recommendation of his scout to watch Ritchie. He raved all the way home to England - not about the player but about the stupidity of his scout bringing him on such a mission.

"The other side of the coin is the Scottish manager who threatened to steep the ball in a bucket of water for two days before the match in the hope that Andy might injure his toes when he took a free kick.

"Big Andy, who was voted Scotland's Footballer of the Year last season, takes it all in his easy stride.

"His philosophy is simple - 'I'm an entertainer and my job is to contribute to the enjoyment of the spectators. I know what I'm not - and don't need to be told. But more important I know what I am and I try to use that to help the team and please the fans'."*

Well please the fans he did during his seven glorious years at Morton.

*Extracts from this programme have been reproduced with the kind permission of the Scottish Football Association.

The Magnificent Seven Alan Finds It Rough! 1980-81

On 1st March 1980, with Celtic six points clear at the top, the League looked like this:

	P	W	L	D	F	A	Pts
Celtic	23	12	3	8	43	21	32
Morton	24	11	9	4	43	35	26
St. Mirren	22	9	6	7	34	34	25
Aberdeen	21	9	7	5	35	25	23
Kilmarnock	22	8	7	7	26	32	23
Rangers	23	9	10	4	34	32	22

With Partick Thistle, both Dundee clubs and Hibernian bringing up the tail end.

Despite being sidelined through injury, Andy Ritchie remained the top Premiership goalscorer with 22 goals.

On Sunday 4th May 1980 at Cappielow Park a testimonial match was held in honour of Hal Stewart. Writing in the testimonial programme the Provost A.O. Fletcher JP says:

"There is no doubt that a successful team locally is not only a good thing for the club itself and its supporters but advantageous to the District as a whole. There is equally no doubt that if it hadn't been for Hal Stewart's energy and enthusiasm when Morton were at their lowest ebb there would be no Morton today.

"It is therefore fitting that this testimonial game should be organised on his behalf as a token of our appreciation for all his hard work. In offering Hal our congratulations we wish him every success for the future."

Lord Westwood, President of the English Football League and of Newcastle United, who like Stewart was born in Dundee, paid his tribute too, as did his Scottish counterpart Tom Lauchlan OBE, who was also chairman of Kilmarnock, and Hugh Taylor, President of the Scottish Football Writers' Association, who called Hal the "Miracle Worker of Clydeside".

Next to Andy Ritchie's thumbnail picture it states how Hal Stewart was responsible for spotting superb talent for Morton, both players from other clubs whose experience kept the club afloat and youngsters who went on to find fame at the highest level. Among them were Joe Harper, Bobby Collins, Allan McGraw, Neil McNab, Joe Jordan and Andy Ritchie, as well as a host of players from Denmark, who are listed under the heading "The Viking Invasion".

One fan did remember that Andy scored in Hal's testimonial, but that has not been confirmed.

Hal Stewart had arrived at Cappielow in 1961 and certainly deserved his 20-year testimonial.

As we know, Hal was responsible for bringing Andy Ritchie to Cappielow from Celtic in that much publicised deal that saw Baines move in the other direction, but he allegedly blocked any move to lure 'The King' away from Morton. Morton fans may thank Haldane Y. Stewart for keeping Andy Ritchie at Greenock, but the player himself may have other thoughts.

Andy Ritchie scored in Hal Stewart's testimonial against Alan Rough, direct from a corner. The strange thing was that Andy had done exactly the same the previous week in a League game.

If nothing else, Mr Ritchie was consistent - consistently great!

On 26th July Morton entertained Albion Rovers in the Dryborough Cup.

The Morton lads, supported by crowd of just short of 3,000, ran out easy winners 4-2, with Thomson (2), Tolmie and Ritchie all on the score sheet. Four days later, however, they went out to Aberdeen by the same score.

In the Anglo Scottish Cup there was some success with a 7-3 aggregate win over Falkirk, but Morton went out to Notts County 3-1 in the next round. In the away leg in England, County ran out 2-0 winners and at Cappielow Andy scored again, but the 1-1 draw was not enough.

Morton fared no better in the Scottish League Cup. Things had looked hopeful when they had a 2-1 away win down the coast at Ayr United, with Ritchie and Hutchison scoring. However, the home leg at Cappielow on 20th August saw Morton lose 2-0 and go out 3-2 on aggregate.

The 1980-81 season in the Premier League kicked off with what was becoming a regular opening game against Celtic at Parkhead. Just under 20,000 saw Andy Ritchie open his account for the season but The Hoops fought back to win 2-1. Celtic would have another terrific season, winning 26 games to finish champions by seven points.

The next three League games were a nightmare, Morton going down 4-1 to St Mirren, drawing at Dundee United and on the end of a 6-0 thrashing at Aberdeen.

September saw Morton bottom of the League and Ritchie hadn't scored since the first League game of the season, although in other competitions he had a total of five goals to his credit.

Morton did pick themselves up in September after the 6-0 drubbing at Pittordrie, achieving two wins. A 2-0 win over Kilmarnock was followed by a visit to Hearts, who were having an even worse time than Morton.

Bobby Moncur, writing in his programme notes, says:

"Two home games without a single League point clearly illustrates the importance of our meeting with Morton this afternoon (20th September 1980).

"The Cappielow men recorded their own first home win last weekend against Kilmarnock by a two goal margin. All our first League points have come from away victories over St Mirren and Kilmarnock. It is of the utmost necessity that we quickly start gathering points in front of our own fans.

"A 1-0 win at Hearts thanks to a McNeil goal."

The players at Tynecastle didn't need any reminder from Moncur, who won the old Inter-City Fairs Cup in his days at Newcastle United. But Moncur disagreed with the local press, who thought Hearts' performances were poor, feeling that their performances had actually been satisfactory. Hearts had lost to Celtic, as indeed had Morton. Moncur pointed out that there were no easy games in the Premier League and urged his players to buckle down. He asked the fans to give the players support and encouragement as Hearts went for the two points.

There were other problems at Tynecastle, as falling attendances were already affecting everyone. A shortage of goals and the presence of hooligans were partly to blame, but the commercial manager Richard Kernick hit the nail on the head in his explanation: "There is so much more to do in the comfort of your own home rather than attending a soccer match on a freezing winter's afternoon." The apparent rise in the birth rate confirmed his suspicions!

Hearts' directors had installed an extra 3,000 seats, but they need not have bothered for that season. Getting bums on seats was never going to happen. The Hearts shop too was stocked with new shirts and team pictures, but disillusionment was the name of the game and most would stay on the shelves.

However, the opposing team always had something to write about Andy Ritchie and their words speak louder than mine: "The immensely talented Ritchie is rated the best striker of a 'dead ball' in Scotland (thanks in part to Rivelino and hours of practice), as several goalkeepers can ruefully testify. He has been Morton's top scorer for the past two seasons and produces patches of skill and vision which can turn a game in seconds."

The writing was on the wall for Bob Moncur, who was capped 16 times by Scotland. Not only did Hearts lose to Morton 1-0, they only won three games at home all season, drawing another three and losing 11, the worst home record in the League. At the end of the season Moncur had to eat a very large slice of humble pie for disagreeing with the press. Hearts would be relegated along with Kilmarnock.

Morton were secure with a nine-point cushion come the end of the year, but Andy Ritchie had not scored a League goal since August despite the fact that he had scored five in Cup competitions. He did manage to get back on target in the home game versus Partick Thistle, but Thistle still won 2-1.

After that game Morton were second from bottom and struggling.

October was marginally better, with a 2-2 draw at home to Rangers, Ritchie scoring again, and a 1-1 draw away to St Mirren. However, two defeats at Airdrie by the odd goal and losing 3-2 to Celtic, with a Ritchie goal, meant that the Cappielow team had only managed to claw up one place to third from bottom.

A marked improvement was needed, otherwise for Andy Ritchie and his teammates it was going to be a very long, hard winter.

Things did improve in November with a 3-1 win at home to Airdrie in which Andy scored a penalty to add to Tolmie and Thomson's strikes. But a 2-0 defeat at home to Dundee United, a goalless draw at Partick and a 2-2 draw at home to Hearts still had Morton in 8th place, just one above the drop zone.

The next two games would test Morton's resolve to the limit and few held out any hope as they visited Ibrox on 29th November.

Before a crowd of just over 17,000, Tolmie netted the only goal. Morton achieved a famous victory and they could now face the mighty Aberdeen side, managed by Alex Ferguson, with renewed confidence.

Mike Jackson, the assistant manager at the time, said, "I'll never forget the day we beat Rangers 1-0 at Ibrox. I don't think we had ever beaten Rangers there in the League. An icy day in November. We had Tolmie and McNeil up front. They slaughtered Rangers and we could have beaten them 3 or 4 nothing. We created so many openings against them. The football that day was tremendous on a tricky pitch." (*Greenock Morton 1874-1999*)

More than 5,300 paid to watch the Aberdeen game and they were not disappointed when Rooney scored the only goal of the game to give Morton victory.

It was the first time in the season that the team recorded three wins on the bounce at home to Airdrie and Aberdeen and the famous away win at Rangers.

The unbeaten run in the League, which had started at Partick on 8th November, continued through December with draws away to Kilmarnock and Hearts and a 2-0 win over Partick Thistle on 27th December.

What looked like being an awful year therefore ended on something of a high, with Morton now up to 6th place in the table.

However, January didn't bring the new hope that Morton fans had anticipated. The team scored only two goals in the month, one from Ritchie and one from Rooney, with three defeats against St Mirren, Celtic and Rangers.

The cloud of relegation was hovering once again over Cappielow.

There was some joy for the team in the SFA Cup, however. Although 0-0 home draw to Hearts appeared to have ended their interest, an against all the odds 3-1 win away from home in the replay saw Morton progress to the fourth round and a home tie with Aberdeen.

The official programme for the away replay on Wednesday 28th January 1981 makes interesting reading, as there is not a single mention of Andy Ritchie, just manager Bob Moncur's expectations that Hearts would finish the job and that the incentive of the prize "should guarantee plenty of action at Tynecastle tonight".

In the 1980-81 season the programme was updated and the previous season's price of 20p was blotted out and replaced with 25p - a 25% increase. These were inflationary times.

When the team had gone to Aberdeen in the League prior to the Cup match on 7th February 1981, they were down to 7th place and many feared the worst. However, the trip north proved worthwhile, a solitary strike from Busby being enough to secure the points before 11,000 fanatical Dons.

The following week Morton welcomed Ferguson's team to Cappielow in the Cup. A crowd of 8,500 welcomed both teams to the arena in what was a battle royal. Andy Ritchie scored his first goal since the penalty on New Year's Day and Morton held on to win 1-0.

Back in the League, a run of three defeats followed as Morton struggled to transfer their Cup form into the Premiership. Defeats at Dundee, Celtic and Airdrie, two by just a 1-0 scoreline, saw Morton slump to 8th in the League.

The Celtic fixture took place on Saturday 28th February at Cappielow Park before a crowd of 13,000 and the programme for that match is particularly special for Andy as it coincided with his 25th birthday - although there wasn't much to celebrate in the 3-1 defeat. Unfortunately, due to the restrictions mentioned earlier, I am unable to reproduce here either the birthday message contained in the programme or the contribution made by the legendary broadcaster Arthur Montford.

When Morton faced Hearts at home on 21st March before a dwindling crowd of just over 3,000, the team were facing the drop. This was a far cry from the first home game of the season against St Mirren, which had attracted 6,700.

Could the team exist financially on crowds that showed a 50% reduction?

However, two goals from 'the rock' McNeil and another from Busby gave the Morton fans something to cheer about. The team moved up one place in the League and fans could breathe a sigh of relief.

Morton supporters' joy was short-lived, however, as the team went down 3-1 at Partick in the next game, the only goal coming from Rooney.

In the remaining five games they had to face Rangers,

Aberdeen and Dundee United and the fans feared the worst.

They lost 4-0 at Ibrox and 3-1 at home to Aberdeen, but took a point away at Kilmarnock before facing Dundee United at home on 18th April. The 2-0 win proved to be the lifeline that The Ton faithful were looking for and momentarily Morton moved up to 7th place. But defeats at St Mirren and at Airdrie, game that had been postponed in January, pulled Morton back to 8th place on 28 points.

However, Andy Ritchie and his teammates had built up a cushion of nine points with results ground out at Hearts, Rangers and Aberdeen and they remained in the Premier League for another season.

Ritchie had scored more than a dozen goals in all competitions for the first team, well supported by his teammates Tolmie, McNeil, Thomson and Rooney. He added six more in the reserves in the six games he played for the second string.

But had some of the magic gone?

In the Cup in the 1980-81 season Morton had much more success.

On 28th January 1981 Morton visited Heart of Midlothian in a Scottish Cup replay. Bob Moncur was quoted at the time as saying he was disappointed that they had failed to eliminate Morton at Cappielow because he thought they deserved a victory. Most of Hearts' chances were beaten out by Roy Baines, who had returned to Morton from his 16-game stint at Celtic.

History was on Hearts' side. Having drawn 3-3 in 1964-65 at Greenock, they went on to win the replay at Tynecastle 2-0. Then in the 1967-68 season, in a Hampden semi-final that finished 1-1, Hearts won the replay 2-1 after extra time. As for Morton, in 1978-79 they had drawn 1-1 at Tynecastle but had lost again 1-0 at home in the replay.

This season the games between the two clubs had resulted in three draws and a narrow 1-0 win for The Ton on 20th September.

Were Hearts going to be the bogey team again?

Not this time, Bobby!

Mr Moncur was made to eat his words and not for the first or last time this season.

Tolmie, Rooney and Thomson netted three times to go through 3-1, silencing the 9,700 home fans. That set up a semi-final encounter in the fourth round with Aberdeen.

There were more than 8,500 in Cappielow on the day and Morton's favourite son did not disappoint, scoring the only goal in a famous 1-0 victory.

Andy Ritchie had done it again.

That set up a quarter-final with Clydebank at Cappielow, which ended 0-0.

Had Morton lost yet another chance to reach a Cup final?

The replay away to Clydebank on 16th March 1981 saw Thomson (3) McNeil, Rooney and Tolmie score six of the best to put Morton through to face Rangers in the semi-final at Parkhead on 11th April before a crowd of 27,000. Morton lost 2-1.

Rangers went on to beat Dundee United 4-1 in the final after a replay.

A total of 96,000 watched the two games and there was a sign that the dwindling crowds would return if they saw goals, goals and more goals.

Morton fans, however, would have exchanged an appearance in the semi-final against Parkhead for more League points ...

Or would they?

The Magnificent Seven
The Cracks Begin to
Show 1981-82

In early August 1981 Morton were engaged in the Scottish League Cup. Four wins and just one defeat and a draw seemed to bode well for the season. They beat Raith Rovers 5-2 and 2-0, Dundee 2-1 and 3-2, had a 1-1 draw with Rangers at home and the only defeat was 1-0 at Ibrox. Thirteen goals scored and just seven conceded.

The League season started with a 2-0 defeat away to St Mirren. They proved to be a bogey team that season, also knocking Morton out of the Scottish Cup 2-1 in the third round.

Back in the League Andy and the boys picked up three wins in September against both Dundee teams and Partick Thistle and were in 4th place as October approached. However, defeats at Aberdeen 2-0, Hibs 4-0 and against that St Mirren team again 2-0 didn't really help Morton's cause, although they did partially recover in a 3-0 win over Airdrie at Cappielow.

By the end of October Morton had slipped from 4th to 7th place. November came and went, the only bright spot being a 1-1 draw with Celtic.

In the whole of December only one League game was possible and Morton made full use of the enforced break by beating Aberdeen 2-1 on 5th December to momentarily occupy 6th place in the League.

Twenty-eight days after the win at home to Aberdeen they

visited St Mirren, on 3rd January 1982, and the lack of match practice showed. Morton lost 3-1 and so it was not the Happy New Year many had hoped for. Morton also met at St Mirren in the FA Cup and again lost, this time 2-1.

Things did improve in February, and a draw with both Aberdeen and Airdrie followed by a 2-0 win at home to Dundee steadied the ship. However, a visit to Ibrox on 27th February proved pointless, resulting in a 3-0 defeat. The following week another trip to Glasgow to play the other 'Old Firm' team was to prove fruitless too. Admittedly it was a much improved performance, Morton losing 1-0 to the eventual champions.

The next three games would prove crucial, and Morton managed to avoid defeat. They beat Airdrie 1-0, drew at Hibs and held Rangers to a goalless draw at Cappielow. However, the rivals at St Mirren once again claimed bragging rights when they came to Cappielow and stole a 1-0 win. Seven days later a 5-0 thrashing at Dundee United did not make pleasant reading for any loyal Morton fan.

But two home games surely would give the fans something to shout about.

On 3rd April champions elect Celtic visited Greenock and the score ended 1-1. The following week saw the same scoreline when Dundee United were the visitors.

The final few weeks of the season were a roller-coaster ride for the Morton faithful. A 4-0 defeat at Partick Thistle was followed by two home wins. Hibs visited on 14th April and lost 2-1. Then three days later Aberdeen came south and returned home pointless (again), losing 2-1. The final four games of the season produced defeats to Dundee and Rangers and draws with Airdrie and Hibs.

From January until the end of the season Morton maintained 7th place, so their Premiership place was secure for at least another season.

Highlights of the rest of the 1981-82 season included wins over Dundee, Airdrie, Hibs and Aberdeen. But nine home wins, 12 draws and no wins away from Cappielow in the

League were never going to be enough to challenge the clubs at the top. In 18 away days they picked up just six points.

Were the cracks beginning to show?

All thoughts of the victories over Aberdeen and Hibernian would become a distant memory for many supporters. But they still held the faith.

They were still in the Premiership. But for how long?

The Magnificent Seven
The End of the Dream
1982-83

There were some matches best forgotten in the 1982-83 season.

On 28th August 1982 Dumbarton were welcomed to Cappielow in the League Cup. With 3-1 win at Dumbarton earlier in the month and a similar success against Dundee, the Morton fans felt another win was on the cards. They were not disappointed and Morton ran out easy winners 4-1, but the attendance sent shivers through the club. Only 1,570 paid to watch the game. Only a year previously in the same competition Cappielow had attracted crowds of 6,000 against Hearts, 8,500 against Aberdeen and 4,792 against Clydebank.

Where were the missing fans?

On 16th October Morton lost 6-0 at Dundee United, who went on to become champions. By the time of the return leg at Cappielow on 18th December, Morton were 13 points behind United in the League. Although the match produced a better result for the home team, Andy was on the bench and Dundee United still won with goals from John Reilly and Paul Sturrock on a hard surface packed with snow.

When Morton visited the bottom club Motherwell on 27th November, manager Alfie Conn was confident that Motherwell could beat the drop.

In the Motherwell programme it says:

"Andy Ritchie needs no introduction to Scottish football fans. The controversial and undoubtedly talented forward was

Morton FC 1979
Back Row: Jim Holmes, Jim Rooney, Jimmy Miller, Roy Baines, Andy Ritchie,
Cammy Melville, George Anderson, Roddie Hutchinson, Ally Scott.
Front Row: John McNeill, Neil Orr, Joe McLaughlin, Bobby Thomson,
Jon Wilkie, Billy MacLaren, Jim Tolmie.

There's only one
Andy Ritchie!
(Photo: Greenock Telegraph)

Andy celebrates: Patrick Thistle v Morton, October 1979

Left: Andy's best ever goal (against Aberdeen), 1981

Below: Andy nutmeg's Rangers centre half

Scottish Premier League

CELTIC
versus
MORTON

Celtic Park

Saturday August 11 1979

Kick-off 3.00 p.m.

15p

PROGRAMME

Left: Celtic v Morton programme, Celtic won 3-2, 11 August 1979

Above: Morton and Scotland fans at The Albert Hotel, Gourock 2007

voted Scotland's Player of the Year four seasons ago and has won international recognition at Scottish League and under 21 level. Andy has superb ball control and has scored some memorable goals. Arguably the most talented player in Scotland."

Andy at this time was 26 years old. His career at Morton would come to an end in the months ahead as he moved to ... Motherwell.

Two wins in the autumn of 1982 were followed by a disastrous run of 12 games without a win up until New Year's Day 1983, when the visitors to Cappielow were Morton's bogey team St Mirren. There was no margin for error.

Well, hope springs eternal and the New Year brought new hope, as Morton beat Mirren 2-0 and followed that with a 3-0 win over Kilmarnock.

Had Morton turned the corner? Could they climb up the table and avoid the drop?

On 26th February 1983 the relegation-threatened Morton team claimed the lead with a Richard Gough goal on 56 minutes, but a fightback ensued and Bobby Hutchinson equalised nine minutes from time.

Morton's demise was almost complete when on 30th April at Tannadice they crashed 4-0 to goals from Davie Dodds (2) Dave Nary and Ralph Milne.

The injection of optimism was short-lived, however, as the lads went another seven games without tasting success. That plunged Morton into 9th place, a position from which they would never recover.

On 14th May 1983 the Morton programme was up 30p and Andy Ritchie had been restored to his number 11 spot. By this time attendance figures at Cappielow were no longer included in the match statistics, but I couldn't have quoted them in any event.

The team did win 3-2 away at St Mirren and recorded another victory at home to Dundee, giving the fans renewed hope, but a subsequent run of six consecutive defeats, during which Morton scored only one goal, spelt disaster.

After five glorious years in the top flight, Morton were relegated along with Kilmarnock. The ten defeats and only six wins all season said it all.

Premier Division Table 1982-83

	P	W	D	L	F	A	Pts
Dundee Utd	36	24	8	4	90	35	56
Celtic	36	25	5	6	90	36	55
Aberdeen	36	25	5	6	76	24	55
Rangers	36	13	12	11	52	41	38
St Mirren	36	11	12	13	47	51	34
Dundee	36	9	11	16	42	53	29
Hibs	36	7	15	14	35	51	29
Motherwell	36	11	5	20	39	74	27
Morton	36	6	8	22	30	74	20
Kilmarnock	36	3	11	22	28	91	17

(Copyright © 1998-2007 Statto Organisation Limited. All rights reserved.)

At the time, in common with many football clubs around the country, everyone was feeling the financial pinch. There was a clear sign that financial problems due to falling attendances could spell the end of Morton's time in the Premier League.

Morton attracted less than 1,600 for the visit of Premier League Motherwell, 1,800 against Hibs and the annual visits from Celtic 12,000 and Rangers 11,000 would not compensate for the missing fans at the 'regular' games.

In the local press, the Morton chairman Hugh M. Currie was reported as saying that the club would have to operate with a reduced first team squad. He believed that some of the blame for what had happened must fall on supporters. He is quoted as saying that it was only money taken through the turnstiles that would help the club.

Of course he was stating the obvious. True supporters go to see their club in the good and bad times and when you are down - well, in the words of that well-known song - "The only way is up".

I have my own views on the financial situation that not only blighted Morton but other clubs as well.

Benny Rooney and his assistant Mike Jackson were made redundant. A total of six top-quality players left the club, including Andy Ritchie. Blaming supporters for not coming through the turnstiles seemed a most un-Morton-like statement for a 'family club'.

Unemployment along the Clyde was running at somewhere between 16% and 20%. For men who were faced with either putting food on the table for their families or paying to watch a football match, well there was no choice.

When the employment situation improved some of the fans returned but the comments of the chairman, however truthful or not, left a bitter taste in many people's mouths.

So the end of the Premiership dream coincided with the end of the Benny Rooney era and the end of Andy Ritchie's loyal seven-year reign as 'King of Cappielow', and the most successful team of all time had been disbanded to balance the books.

Jim Tolmie, Bobby Thomson and Neil Orr all ended up with moves away from the club, some of them big money ones. However, Andy went to Motherwell for a mere £35,000-£50,000.

Andy had allegedly been denied a big money move and years later it transpired that Nottingham Forest, Everton, Watford, Liverpool and a host of other clubs had made a move for the prolific striker. Pre-Bosman, however, he was never told of this interest, which could have made him financially comfortable.

The heart had apparently gone out of Andy Ritchie.

Jock Stein had given him away on a free transfer because of their much publicised spats. Then as manager of the national side Jock had only taken Andy along to a Euro Qualifier because of the pressure applied by the SFA, where he was thrown the crumbs from the top table with an over-age Under-23 cap.

Benny Rooney and his assistant were made redundant by a

board who said they could no longer afford the pair. The club reported a loss of £4,350 per week.

So Andy's love affair with the fans of Greenock Morton was over and 'The King of Cappielow' abdicated and moved to Motherwell.

These were sad times indeed for everyone associated with the club, very sad times.

Greenock Morton, as we have seen, have had several ups and downs. However, there are signs that under the stewardship of Mr Douglas Rae, the current chairman, a return to the Premier League is not beyond the realms of possibility.

The fans today, as in 1983, have an important part to play in the revival and their support in 2006-07 was crucial in Morton's return to the First Division.

Next stop the Premiership?

Misery at Motherwell

Information pertaining to Andy Ritchie's time at Motherwell was, at best, incomplete. However, thanks to the co-operation of Graham Barnstaple at the club, accurate statistics give a full account. Graham has a private collection of Motherwell programmes, and his contribution to Andy's story and time at Motherwell has been invaluable.

Andy played eight League games for Motherwell, including six starts, and he scored in an historic win at Ibrox against Rangers, slotting home a penalty in a 2-1 win. After that defeat John Grieg was sacked and Jock Wallace took over at Rangers.

Andy also played eight League Cup games, starting in seven. Motherwell beat Berwick Rangers 2-0 home and away to set up matches in the group stages.

On 31st August 1983, Andy played against his former club Morton. The Motherwell programme, which contains a photograph of Andy in a Motherwell shirt in which he looks extremely unhappy, records that Andy was signed for £27,000, had proved a big hit with the Fir Park faithful and hoped to make a big impact against his former teammates from Greenock - which he did, scoring in the 3-0 win and also again in a 4-2 defeat at Cappielow. However, some records say that he only scored once - in August 1984 at Fir Park in a Motherwell victory. Motherwell also beat Alloa to edge into 2nd place behind group winners Dundee United. Morton finished bottom of the group.

There was a great deal of depression around Scottish football and in this programme Motherwell explain their slant on the crisis:

"Last season we appealed to local companies and to local people in better circumstances to consider helping those people who can no longer afford to come and see Motherwell play."

Unemployment in Scotland in 1982-83 had a profound effect on the League attendances.

In 1982 the number of people unemployed in Britain topped the three million mark for the first time since the 1930s, and in Scotland unemployment in adult males was 16% compared with less than 10% in the south-east of England. There were 750,000 long-term unemployed and Labour Party Leader Michael Foot claimed that there were 32 people chasing every job, so for many young people it was impossible to find work (Source: Government employment statistics.)

There were sporadic outbreaks of violence such as the riots in Toxteth, Liverpool, in July 1981, which many felt were partly to blame for the high level of unemployment in the area.

Scotland was suffering more than most and this was reflected in the drop in attendances.

Former Motherwell supporter Tom Gallagher, when speaking about Andy Ritchie some 12 years later, concluded that it was the last of someone very special, the last of the great soccer heroes.

The current manager at Motherwell is Mark McGhee who was a teammate of Andy's at Cappielow before going on to greater things. Mark played 64 times for Morton, scoring 37 goals before he moved to Newcastle United. He played 28 games for the Magpies, scoring five goals before a move back to Scotland with Aberdeen who, as mentioned earlier, had also considered taking Andy, but opted for Mark instead.

Mark's greatest moment came in 1983 when he was in the Aberdeen side that defeated Real Madrid to lift the European Cup Winners' Cup. He moved on to Hamburg, netting seven goals in 30 games, then came back home to Scotland with Celtic, scoring another 27 goals in 88 games, before returning to Newcastle United for two seasons, where he scored 24 goals in 67 games before having a flirtation with IK Brage, where he scored two goals in three outings. Finally, before his retirement in 1993, he joined Reading, where he scored seven times in 45 games.

In 1982 McGhee won the Scottish PFA Players' Player of the Year award as well as four international caps with Scotland, for whom he scored twice. His managerial career has been a roller-coaster ride, with jobs at Reading, Leicester City, Wolves, Millwall, Brighton and currently at Motherwell, not too far from his birthplace in Glasgow.

Andy Ritchie was about the same age as Mark, but Andy's career ended eight years earlier than his - too early in many pundits' opinions.

Andy's time at Motherwell had been miserable and the deposed king was in danger of become totally disillusioned. The happier times at Morton had quickly become a distant dream, and in less than five years he had moved from being Scotland's Player of the Year to oblivion.

It was time to move on.

Next stop Albion Rovers but first a trip to Hanover.

In the 1980s, as Andy tried to reconcile his love affair with football in a career that was to take him from the dizzy heights of Celtic Park eventually to Albion Rovers, Andy ended up in Germany.

He went to Hanover on a three-week trial, the German club hoping that Andy would form a strike partnership with a player called Schneider. However, that never transpired and Schneider was sold to Hamburg. Mark McGhee also played for Hamburg for a while before returning to Scotland.

Andy returned home from Germany a little disillusioned with life. He had been denied a career at Celtic, given a free transfer to Morton, denied a big money move from Greenock and denied an international cap, despite pressure from the fans and the Scottish Football Association.

He had every right to be disillusioned if not bitter, but the word bitter is not in Andy Ritchie's vocabulary.

Everyone you meet describes Andy as 'a nice guy', and that's my impression of him too.

Rover and Out!
But I Found Another
Legend

So Andy Ritchie moved from Motherwell to take up a job with Albion Rovers, seemingly feeling somewhat disillusioned with football.

That may be so, but on a positive note Andy was allegedly responsible for kick-starting the career of another player at Rovers who was in the doldrums and who would go on to become a legend - Bernie Slaven.

Andy claims that he approached Bernie and persuaded him that he could do a job for Albion Rovers similar to the one he had done at Morton. Unlike the scenario he had gone through himself, Andy promised Bernie that he would let him go on a big money move - to England as it transpired. True to his word, Andy encouraged Bernie to move south to Middlesbrough, where he was to become a legend.

However, some claim that Bernie refused to sign a contract at Rovers and instead took a part-time job as a gardener and in this interim period wrote to every First Division and Second Division club in England, his only response coming from Middlesbrough.

The late Willie Maddren, former Middlesbrough manager, had a different version of events as well, in which he claimed responsibility for bringing 'Wolfman', as Bernie became known by the fans, to Ayresome Park.

I was so fascinated by the many stories circulating in regard to this that I decided to contact Bernie Slaven directly and, in late December, on a freezing cold morning in the north-east of England, I eventually tracked down the Wolfman, not by following his footprints in the snow but by arranging to meet him in the most civilised surroundings of the Tall Trees Motel, near Yarm in North Yorkshire.

Bernie Slaven is a legend in the north-east, not only from his days playing for Middlesbrough but also because he is part of the 'Three Legends', a radio show broadcast every weekday evening in the region. His two pals on the show are Malcolm McDonald of Newcastle United and Mick Horswill, late of Sunderland, who replaced Eric Gates. He formed a working partnership with Alistair Brownlee, his commentary partner, and they won an award in New York for their commentary on Middlesbrough's UEFA Cup exploits in the 2005-06 season.

In 2002 he actually ran for Mayor of Middlesbrough, although he admits he knows very little about politics. The result was inevitable and he lost to 'Robo Cop', Ray Mallon. Well it had to be someone of that ilk to beat the gritty Scot.

But of course Bernie is not from England, as his soft accent reveals. He was born on 13th November 1960 in Paisley, Scotland.

Bernie spent a couple of years at Greenock Morton, between 1981 and 1983, after graduating from Celtic Boys Club and played a few times with Andy Ritchie, whom he calls 'Huggy' after Huggy Bear from a popular television series at that time, *Starsky and Hutch*. His days at Morton were not particularly successful as history now tells us - they were playing him out of position. Bernie played as right half and was great going forward, but as a defender, well, Mr Slaven could not defend - his words not mine. Bernie describes himself as a 'fringe player', something he would never be at Boro.

Bernie left Morton in 1983 after just one goal in 22 starts. He then played twice for Airdrie and twice for Queen of the South before contemplating packing it in altogether.

However, on his return from a holiday in Spain, Bernie was informed by his father that Andy Ritchie had been to see him. Bernie contacted Andy, who told him that he would like him to come to Albion Rovers, where he was by that time player/manager, and do for Rovers what Andy had done for Morton. Bernie accepted the invitation.

As left half at Albion Rovers, Bernie was given a similar role to the one that Andy had occupied at Morton. Bernie was an instant success and went on to play 42 games for Albion Rovers, scoring an incredible 27 goals. At the end of the season Bernie won The Daily Record Golden Boot Award and collected a crate of champagne.

By this time Andy Ritchie had moved on, to be replaced by Joe Baker, the former Arsenal and Hibs hero, but never one to be tagged greedy Bernie Slaven sought out his former mentor and presented Andy Ritchie with one of the bottles of champagne. His next stop was the local hospital to visit a player, Jim Beacon, who had broken a leg. Jim was not allowed alcohol in the ward but some how Bernie was able to skip past the nurses as he had done with so many defenders that season.

Andrew Gold, a reporter with the *Weekly News*, suggested to Bernie that he should circulate his CV and availability to all the top clubs in England, and as a result Middlesbrough signed him in 1985. Bernie was signed from Albion Rovers for £25,000 and is considered by many to be the best buy Middlesbrough ever made, knocking in 146 goals in 381 appearances whilst playing in his famous number 7 shirt, including 119 in the League, and his scoring exploits earned him a call-up to Jack Charlton's Republic of Ireland squad in the 1990 World Cup in Italy.

Jack had researched Bernie's ancestry, as he had done with so many other players, and had quickly discovered that, although born in Scotland, he had Irish roots. Bernie's mam was born in Co. Donegal, Southern Ireland, and his dad in Northern Ireland. He could have played for either country. Bernie chose the emerald green of his mother's homeland although, after discussions with Andy Roxburgh at one time, he could have played for the 'Tartan Army' as well. Bernie played for the Republic of Ireland on seven occasions, scoring one goal.

In the 1990 World Cup, in the group stages, Ireland finished second to England in Group F with a 1-1 draw over England, a 0-0 draw with Egypt and a 1-1 draw with Holland. In the second round Holland went out 2-1 to West Germany, but Ireland progressed against Romania 5-4 on penalties after a 0-0 draw. England beat Belgium in Bologna and both Ireland and England progressed to the quarter-finals, where Ireland lost 1-0 to the hosts in Rome and England beat Cameroon 3-2 in Naples, setting up a semi-final clash with old rivals West Germany. The score was 1-1 in the England game, with Germany winning on penalties to face and beat Argentina, including Maradona, in the final in Rome 1-0, with a penalty from Brehme. England lost the third place play-off to hosts Italy 2-1, the Schillaci penalty winning it for the Italians. Yes, it was the World Cup of penalties.

Back at Boro in his number 7 shirt, Bernie continued his scoring spree until 1992. Goalkeeper Steve Pears said he didn't strike the ball into the net, he passed it. In his seven-and-a-half years at Middlesbrough the Wolfman experienced all the high and lows that this north-east club had to offer.

In his second year at Middlesbrough, 1986, Bernie experienced relegation for the first time, but the man was not for quitting. Bruce Rioch took over at the helm and steered Boro to promotion, with Bernie playing a full part the following year in 1987. And things got even better in the following season, when successive promotions brought the crowds back to Boro. The 1989 season brought disappointment, however. The club were relegated and the rock in the defence, Gary Pallister, was sold to Manchester United.

In 1990 Rioch was sacked to be replaced by Colin Todd, and he led Boro to Wembley for the first time. Bernie scored a crucial goal in the Zenith Data Systems Cup against Aston Villa to book their place in the final and Boro's first ever trip to Wembley. In the final Boro met Chelsea in a close-fought battle and Chelsea won 1-0.

In 1991 Bernie's goals were crucial again in helping Boro to reach the play-off semi-finals, but they came out losers. Manager Todd was then replaced by Lennie Lawrence.

1992, the inaugural season of the Premier League, saw Middlesbrough promoted to take their place alongside top-flight clubs such as Manchester United and Liverpool.

In 1993 Boro were to be relegated again in what had become a regular love affair with the Premier League. Bernie went back to Wembley with Middlesbrough, scoring in a 2-1 win over Stockport County in the Auto Glass Trophy, but his days were numbered. He is thought to have had words with Lennie Lawrence and the legend left Teesside, subsequently plying his trade at Port Vale and Boro's near neighbours Darlington and scoring goals for both.

I recently watched a DVD of Bernie's goals, owned by my good pal David Wheatley from Stokesley. He and his wife Pam have been Boro fans for years. They kindly took me as their guest to the Riverside Stadium to see the great Juninho play.

But how did David rate Bernie's contribution to Middlesbrough Football Club? Here's what he said:

"Bernie Slaven was one of the most direct strikers in the game. I would compare him to Malcolm McDonald, a powerful bulldozer of a centre forward, head down and full steam ahead, finishing with a piledriver of a shot with either foot. He was a lethal finisher who turned many a half chance into a goal.

"No wonder he is revered as a legend, the all-action 'Bernie the Bolt', great value, never a dull moment when Bernie was on the ball.

"In 1996, a year after he said farewell to Quakers fans, Bernie said on live radio with Century FM that if Middlesbrough beat Manchester United at Old Trafford he would perform a dare. If the Boro won he would 'bare his backside in Binns' window'. Binns has a large department store in the centre of Middlesbrough and such an act would attract large crowds and maybe a discount from the House of

Frazer for Bernie.

"Manchester United 2 Middlesbrough 3 was the final score. So, true to his word, Bernie Slaven went ahead with the dare. With the score painted on his rosy cheeks, he stood as he had been born 36 years earlier in Binns' window. You could not move for admirers!

"From that day he says he became known as 'Big Bernie'. The rest I will leave to your imagination!"

When it was time for Bernie to move on, he was approached by several clubs. Bolton (under his former boss at Boro, Bruce Rioch), West Brom (under Ossie Ardilles) and Forest were all thought to be interested in capturing his signature. After all, he was a proven goalscorer.

The unlikely winners in the race for Slaven's signature were Potteries club Port Vale. They were the only club that offered a longer contract - longer than the end of the season, that is.

Port Vale reached the play-offs in his first season, 1992-93, but the team first had an appearance at Wembley on 22nd May 1993 when they picked up the Auto Glass Trophy, beating Stockport County 2-1. They also beat County by the same score to reach Wembley again, but this time they lost 3-0 to West Bromwich Albion. Also in that season they were drawn at home to the then top-flight Southampton and Port Vale ran out winners 1-0 - a Premiership scalp for the underdogs. They would draw Wolves in the next round and lose 2-0. At the end of the 1993-94 season, Port Vale were promoted as runners-up.

Bernie's contribution to the club was nine goals in 33 appearances. Once again he had delivered the goods. Bernie then moved to Darlington where 37 appearances would yield seven goals and mark the end of his playing career.

He then moved on to become a legend on the radio and has produced several books, including his fascinating autobiography *Legend?*, via the publishing company he formed with Alistair Brownlee.

But all this history might never have seen the light of day if Mr Andy Ritchie had not called at Bernie's dad's house and invited Bernie 'Wolfman' Slaven to join him at Albion Rovers.

These are the true facts as told to me by Bernie.

One legend, Andy Ritchie, creating another legend, Bernie Slaven.

Magic.

Andy and Bernie are still good friends and meet as often as they can, usually at some football function in Scotland.

Maybe if Jack Charlton had been the Republic of Ireland manager between 1976 and 1983 he would have researched Andy Ritchie's proud family history and might have discovered a great, great, great-grandfather had come from County Cork.

Was there a Jack O'Ritchie in Ireland who emigrated to Scotland?

We shall never know.

But that would have been something to see - Ritchie playing in the Republic colours.

The Call of the Capital
The World of
Football's Loss

At the age of just 27 years Andy Ritchie, the Idle Idol, the Ambling Alp, Huggy Bear, the self-styled 'King of Cappielow' disappeared from the fields he had graced in the Scottish Leagues.

Andy went south to London.

He began studying as a mature student at North London Polytechnic on a Business Management Course. In order pay the fees and complete the course he took on several part-time jobs, including one as a parking attendant.

Scotland's Player of the Year 1979 was now out of football altogether and parking cars. What a disgrace!

He graduated with honours from the Polytechnic and was successful in obtaining a post as assistant manager at the Barbican Centre in London, where he remained for three to four years. So he ended up with a good job in the capital with an excellent salary and his boys were receiving a brilliant education at a top London school. Andy's wife also had a good job working as an optician and the family enjoyed a very comfortable lifestyle in a beautiful home.

During his employment at the Barbican Andy regularly rubbed shoulders with the rich and famous at the theatre as well as in the West End. One week it would be the Royal Shakespeare Company, the next Tony Bennett, followed by Barbara Dixon. The Barbican attracted the cream of the entertainment world - including, it would seem, Andy Ritchie.

However, despite all this, Andy missed football every day of his life, as well as his homeland, Scotland, where he yearned to return.

On a visit to Bellshill to see his parents, Andrew and Bessie, he met an old acquaintance, Jimmy Dempsey, who was at Hamilton Academicals. Jimmy offered Andy the assistant manager's job at Accies.

Andy didn't need asking twice.

He gave up his luxurious lifestyle in London, uprooted his family and moved back to Scotland.

Coming Home
Return of the King

So Andy was now back in Scotland as assistant manager at Hamilton.

He recalls one day meeting John Wilson, a lifelong Morton supporter, who told him he was thinking of buying Morton Football Club. Mr Wilson was retiring from his lucrative ship-dredging business on the River Clyde and was looking to reinvest his millions. At first Andy thought the Morton supporter was spinning a yarn but, true to his word, John Wilson bought the club.

A return to Morton Football Club for Andy seemed to be on the cards.

Andy was interviewed at Buchanan Toffees by Douglas Rae, who later became owner of Morton Football Club. A contract was finally signed and Andy arrived at Cappielow to meet the manager, Alan McGraw, who had not been advised of the board's decision to offer Andy the post of assistant manager. He was furious, and it placed both former Morton greats in a difficult and embarrassing situation.

Alan advised Andy Ritchie that if he were considering appointing an assistant manager it certainly would not be him, it would be Jackie McNamara snr. He explained that he felt Andy posed a threat to his position, as if he lost three games in a row the crowd would be shouting for Ritchie to be appointed manager.

At the time Andy Ritchie did not make these facts public because he respected Alan McGraw and the contribution he had made at Morton Football Club.

John Wilson continued to pay Andy for six months and Andy

admitted that there was very little he could do - because he wasn't wanted at Morton.

One can only imagine how the deposed 'King' must have felt at the time: unwanted, useless and with nowhere to go.

Andy wanted to work at Morton, but he acknowledged that Alan McGraw did a terrific job. The club shouldn't have appointed Ritchie without discussing the situation with McGraw first. It was not the best public relations exercise in the world! But then, from my own dealings with the club, public relations still need some attention.

Alan McGraw was brutally honest in his discussion with Andy and Ritchie respected his honesty. He still sees Alan at sportsmen's dinners and social events and still holds him in high regard.

So Andy Ritchie left Morton for a second time, as realistically there wasn't a job for him. So, as if the first departure wasn't miserable enough, this second departure left him feeling even more miserable. It had taken him out of football - again.

Andy Ritchie went to work for a chemical company in Glasgow initially to help out an old friend. He'd had some experience at selling, having been a lottery executive in Morton as well as a player. In truth, Andy could sell the proverbial ice cream to Eskimos. Some four years later Andy was still up to his neck in the chemical business.

It was at that point that his friend decided that, as the business was now on the up, he would sell out and it was taken over by one of the largest competitors in Scotland. Andy's pal had made enough money to at 53, partially thanks to Andy's contribution.

Andy was once again seeking employment.

The club that had once given him a free transfer to Morton after one too many spats with the legendary Jock Stein came to his rescue. Tommy Burns asked Andy if he would help out at Parkhead and Andy assumed responsibility for running the youth team.

So, having spent seven years at Morton as a player and five

years at Celtic, Andy Ritchie had now become a journeyman on the managerial roundabout.

Andy had a spell as assistant manager at St Mirren under Jimmy Bone, working alongside two qualified coaches at the club, Campbell Money and Kenny McDowall. Campbell had been at Ayr United and Kenny at Ibrox. On a match day the two coaches were reluctant to stand next to Andy in the dugout, because of the abuse hurled in his direction from the St Mirren fans, who remembered the many times Andy had scored against their club, and feelings ran very high when they had their backs against the wall.

Andy then continued his journey as a scout at Celtic, Aston Villa and other clubs before obtaining his current position as a Scottish Premier League delegate.

The SPL job involves observing all aspects of the game, the dugouts, changing rooms, racist chants - in fact everything that makes up the colourful canvas of a Premier League game. He then submits his report to the SPL.

Andy may well have simplified the contribution he makes to the beautiful game today, but at least he remains involved in football.

'The King of Cappielow' may well have lost his crown almost 25 years ago when he left Morton, but he is still held in high regard by his 'subjects' in Greenock.

Together Again
Andy and Alan Back
on the Same Team

Greenock Morton Supporters Society Limited
A Branch of the Green Oak Tree
   Andy Ritchie and Allan McGraw have come together again in the interest of Greenock Morton Football Club. The two Cappielow legends have once again joined forces to support the Supporters' Trust.
   Foreword by Andy Ritchie and Allan McGraw
   Written by Ryan Deegan
   4th June 2007

Andy Ritchie
"It's great to see the Morton fans rally and take a big step forward in securing the future of the club. When I heard what the Trust was all about I was only too happy to pledge my support. I have many great memories playing for the Ton and the support that the fans gave to the team in my heyday was second to none.

   "I try to get to Cappielow as often as I can and I know only too well the depression that has been hanging over the club these past few years. Other troubled football clubs, particularly in England, have set up Supporters' Trusts recently and this seems to be the way ahead for smaller community-based clubs. Not that Morton are a small club of course. We have the potential to be back up there in the top flight of Scottish football and I'm sure the Supporters' Trust will help towards getting us there. All I can ask is for you to support the Trust as much as you have supported the club over the years. If you do that, then I'm confident there is a bright future ahead for us all."

Allan McGraw

"Next to my family, Morton Football Club has been the most important thing to me in my life.

"The last few years have been a traumatic time for everyone connected with the club, which culminated in the form of the protest rally and march in May of this year in protest against the previous regime at Cappielow. It was a privilege to speak at the rally along with organiser and Morton fan Jim McColl, who has recently pleaded the Morton case with parliamentarians after the previous chairman threatened to close the club 'just like the shipyards'.

"I had begun to despair about the future of the club until I heard about the Supporters' Trust, which I'm sure is the way ahead to secure the long-term future of Morton FC. I know that Jim and Trust organiser Stuart Duncan and his team have put in a power of work behind the scenes to bring the idea of the Trust to reality. At the rally in May I spoke about the fans being the saviours of the club and that opportunity has now arrived. In my long association with the club I have seen managers, players, coaches and office staff come and go - myself included! But it's YOU, the supporters, that have always been there through thick and thin. YOU are the people who care more than anyone. YOU are the lifeblood of Greenock Morton Football Club.

"Now you are being given the chance to have a real say in the future of YOUR club. By joining the Greenock Morton Supporters' Trust we can all work together to secure a brighter and better future for the club. Collectively we can be the saviours of our club and I would urge you all to join the Trust."

- Greenock Morton Supporters' Trust

The appeal from Andy Ritchie and Allan McGraw certainly worked. Well, it did in my case. I am now a member of the Greenock Morton Supporters' Trust and a shareholder at Cappielow.

What the People Say

During Andy Ritchie's career, which lasted just 12 short years, there were many millions of words written about his genius.

Following his glory days at Morton, it would appear that he lost his appetite for the game. Well, he may have appeared to have forgotten about the game, but the people who wrote about game just couldn't get enough.

His adoring fans at Cappielow continued to talk about his fantastic skill and impossible goals and they still do today, almost 25 years after he retired.

This is an attempt to draw together many of the comments that have been made about Andy Ritchie, in addition to the quotes and observations included earlier in the book, into a definitive reference. Some either have not been previously seen or have not been mentioned for decades, and they includes anecdotes from family, friends, colleagues, the media, players, managers and the fans from Cappielow.

There is no doubt that somebody will declare that one important quote has been omitted and that is indeed possible, as so many words have been written, quotes uttered and stories told about the legend of 'The King of Cappielow'.

The most recent accolade is contained in the foreword to this book, written by Sir Alex Ferguson CBE, a man who has done it all, seen it all and continued to make Manchester United probably the most famous club in the world - outside of Glasgow that is.

Graeme Ross, a fellow author, who penned a chapter on Andy in his book *Morton Greats* met with myself and Andy Ritchie on 1st December 2007 after Morton's 2-2 draw with Livingston at Cappielow. Graeme has kindly allowed me to reproduce the chapter on Andy Ritchie from his book. The chapter is simply entitled 'Genius':

Let's nail the myth straight away. Andy Ritchie was a team player. 137 goals and countless assists in seven seasons at Morton tell us so. And lest there is any doubt, many of his team mates tell us so too. Newspaper editors love to pigeonhole players. That's why Andy was a gift for journalists who unfairly dubbed him the 'idle idol'. When Sir Alex Ferguson described Andy as 'an overweight genius' in his autobiography, it was typical of the backhanded comments that have haunted Andy throughout his playing career, and indeed subsequently. Andy himself is tired of the clichéd portrayal that unimaginative writers have attached to him. As Benny Rooney, the man who brought him to Cappielow, says, 'The idle idol reputation was a bit unfair. When I had Andy on his own he was a good trainer, it was only in a group situation that he lapsed a little'.

Perhaps the time is now right for a reassessment of Andy's career. Andy Ritchie was a supremely gifted individual who triumphed in a team game. He was at once part of the team, but his wonderful talent elevated him to a much higher plane. He had it all. He was a giant of a man, but his balance, ball control, passing ability and shooting prowess were unsurpassed. Okay, he didn't run about any more than he had to, and he didn't tackle an awful lot. So what? He didn't have to. Call him a maverick if you like, but his lineage can be traced through all the great Scottish players from Hughie Gallacher to Jim Baxter. Like them, he had that touch of arrogance and faith in his own ability that set him apart from other mere mortals.

Andy Ritchie was born in 1956 in Glasgow and spent his early life in the Calderpark region. His family later moved to Bellshill and as Andy's father was a Motherwell supporter, he took young Andy to a lot of their matches. The excellent sides of the late 1960's, including John Martis, Bobby and Willie McCallum and John Goldthorpe, were his early heroes. On leaving school, Andy's chosen career path was mining engineering, a path which very quickly me a dead end, as he realised it wasn't for him. Football was his passion. He played for his school team, where Craig Brown was his headmaster, and juvenile for Bellshill YM.

Basically like most other young lads I just played football all the time. If I couldn't rustle up a game with other kids, I'd be away by myself, always with a ball. I suppose I was born with a bit of a gift, but I was always working on my technique and ability. Not only that, in my head as well. I believe that a big percentage of football is played in your head, and I had a vivid imagination. I also lived near Jimmy Johnstone, remember, so he was always a reminder of what could be achieved.

Andy was 14 when he first realised that football clubs were interested in him. He played trials with Manchester United, Coventry and Everton, and spent two months with Middlesbrough.

I was homesick in Middlesbrough after three days, and through the grapevine I heard Celtic were interested. As a kid you have hopes and dreams and aspirations that one day you'll be good enough, but deep down you never really think that will happen. It always happens to someone else. I was a bit of a late starter. English clubs used to hold trials up here, and all the scouts would organise the best boys and hold trials on a Sunday. Clubs like West Brom, Crystal Palace and Leeds would be there. I was never, ever invited to any of those trials. Three guys from my team Bellshill YM were there one day, but there was a man short that day, and my dad told me to go along and make the numbers up. After 20 minutes I was taken off, and I got back on for the last 15 minutes. I only found out years later that the reason I'd been taken off after 20 minutes was the Middlesbrough coach was there and he knew the place was hoachin' with scouts and wanted me out of their sight. Middlesbrough had the first option on me and that was the reason I was taken off. I just thought I'd been having a poor game. It was almost as if Benny Rooney was the manager and the number 11 board was being held up.....again! But at the end of the match before I got to the car park I'd been approached by Manchester United and Celtic scouts, and by the time I got home the Rangers scout was in my mother's house.

Andy chose not to go back to Middlesbrough, but still had his pick of the big clubs. 'I could have signed for Rangers. I was training with them on a Tuesday night and Celtic on a Thursday, but I went to Celtic because they were more organised, their structure was better'.

Andy joined the Celtic ground staff in 1971 aged 15, and followed the then tried and tested route of being farmed out to junior football. In Kenny Dalglish's case is was Cumbernauld United. Andy went to Kirkintilloch Rob Roy. There he made a huge impression, scoring 35 goals in 18 matches, including five in his first match. At 17 Andy signed professional forms for Celtic, and he made an immediate impact in the reserves. Everything was happening quickly for Andy, but in retrospect he thinks it may have been too quick.

I wasn't achieving anything mentally, I wasn't growing up mentally. Physically yes, mentally no. I then hit a brick wall and didn't know how to fix it. I believed I should have been in the first team, but my high expectations weren't backed up by my performances. I developed an attitude and wouldn't do what I was told. There was a two-year spell which wasn't good. All I needed was a tad of humility, but it was the arrogance of youth. If Jock Stein had been there he might have sorted me out. But he had been in a car crash and Parkhead was in turmoil without him. Players were leaving and I thought I was better than the replacements. When Jock did come back I had lost focus.

Andy managed half a dozen appearances in 1975-76, but in October 1976 he took the decision to move to Morton.

Benny (Rooney) had only just stopped playing, and I remember playing against him a couple of times, and he obviously remembered me. He was very persuasive and sold Morton to me. Of course, I could have stayed at Celtic. There was a four-year deal on the table from Celtic, and I turned it down. Bad, bad, bad move!

Of the many myths that have grown up around Andy, one of the strongest is of his love/hate relationship with Jock Stein.

All that stuff with big Jock has been exaggerated a bit. For his part I think it was more frustration at my attitude. I had that arrogant side to me and I couldn't be told. He rated me as a player, and was always trying to get me back into the fold. There was nothing Jock didn't know and nothing he couldn't do. Right up until the day I signed for Morton he tried to get me to stay. Can you imagine it? A four-year deal on the table, and I turned down possibly the greatest Scottish manager ever. I'll never forget when he finally gave up on me. He gave a disgusted aaargch! Shrugged his shoulders and walked out of the room.

Andy came to Morton just at the right time. The club had steadily gone downhill since the halcyon days of the 1960's, and had failed to gain a place in the promised land that was the much vaunted Premier League. Enter Benny Rooney, a dynamic, ambitious young manager who would galvanise a stagnating club, and for an all too brief period give Morton fans a team to be proud of. Benny had been at Morton for just a few months when he put feelers out for Andy. Celtic, as always seemed to be the case after Ronnie Simpson retired, were looking for a goalkeeeeper. Roy Baines had been outstanding for Morton for several seasons. Roy moved to Parkhead and Andy came the other way as makeweight in the deal. Morton also received £10,000. The last part is worth repeating, Morton received £10,000. Celtic were actually giving Morton money to take Andy Ritchie off their hands. Now Roy Baines is indisputably one of Morton's best ever goalkeepers, arguably second only to Jimmy Cowan, but Benny Rooney must have been rubbing his hands in glee at the thought of bringing Andy to Cappielow. But could Benny have known just how great a signing it would turn out to be?

Andy was the most talented player that I ever managed. He could do everything. When I took over at Morton I had a team full of workers and I signed Andy to give us that extra something. I wanted him on the ball making things happen.

And he certainly did that for us. For three or four seasons he was incredible. His dead ball skills and passing ability were second to none. He really was the cream on the cake.

Andy made a fairly quiet Morton debut in October at Cappielow against Clydebank. He impressed with his dribbling and close control, which were excellent for such a big guy. He also gave a sign of things to come with a couple of free kicks that were capably dealt with by the Bankies goalie. A few of the Cappielow cognoscenti reckoned he was a star of the future, and by the time of his next home match when he scored two goals against Montrose, few were in any doubt that he was a star of the present. His double against Montrose included one direct from a free kick. Up until then, most Scottish fans' exposure to free-kick goals was via grainy black and white images from the 1970 Mexico World Cup, when Pele, Rivelino et al had held us spellbound into the wee hours of the morning.

I always knew that I had talent for striking the ball in a certain way, and I would spend time after training practising my passing and hitting free kicks. I went over to Germany in 1974 to support Scotland in the World Cup, and I happened to catch a Brazilian training session. And that was all they were doing, hitting free kick after free kick. And they had this big cardboard wall, the first time I had seen anything like it, and they were swerving the ball around it. Just sitting there watching them made me wish I could get on the park with them.

And so, working on the old adage, 'If you can't join them, beat them', free kicks became an integral part of Andy's game. Over his seven years at Morton he would frequently astonish fans, team mates, and opponents alike with his astonishing dead ball prowess.

In his first season at Cappielow Benny Rooney moulded a promising side around the talents of Andy. A tremendous unbeaten run of games secured them fourth place in the League, and Andy finished with 22 goals in 27 appearances. 'I had several seasons of full-time training behind me, and when

I joined Morton I was as fit as I've ever been, and so I hit the ground running'. But Morton fans were unaware that they had been close to losing their new hero soon after his arrival.

I'd only played eight games for Morton, and Celtic were willing to pay up to £175,000 to bring me back on the proviso that Morton took the money and said I'd only been at Cappielow on loan. But Hal Stewart said no, I'll get a million for him, and that was that.

The start of the 1977-78 season saw Hearts and Dundee installed as favourites for promotion. Both sides were full-time and more fashionable than part-time Morton. But no one read the script to Morton players. They dominated the League from day one, with the Ritchie/Mark McGhee combination on fire, and Andy was thrilled to play alongside his old hero John Goldthorpe. The football was terrific with Andy as chief conductor.

My brief was just get on the ball and make the team play. Benny Rooney at that time was one of the best young managers in the game. He had good contacts in the game and knew what he wanted, and he knew Scottish football. I got the feeling after a couple of months that something was happening. He gave me more or less a free role, within reason. I just went out to enjoy myself, make the team play, and tried to entertain.

One of the more memorable matches in the season 1977-78 was at Cappielow against Hearts. There was an air of expectancy around the ground as the sides took the field. Hearts had comprehensively defeated 'Ton in the League Cup only three days previously, and this was to be the game where the Edinburgh aristocrats would put the poor relations from Greenock in their place, and finish their challenge. It didn't quite work out like that as Morton took the game to Hearts from the off, and produced a scintillating display of attacking football. Morton led 3-0 at half time, and the match was effectively over. Well not quite, as Hearts quickly pulled two goals back after the interval, but Morton were not to be denied and, from a Ritchie corner, the much maligned Roddy

Hutchison bulleted a header past the Hearts goalie. Morton made it 5-2 before Hearts pulled a third goal back near the end.

A jubilant Morton side and supporters celebrated a performance that signalled that Benny Rooney's side had come of age. The most surprising thing about the match was the absence of Andy's name from the score sheet, but the most significant factor was that he had set up four of Morton's goals, proving that when he played a deeper role he could be just as effective. Morton never looked back after this match and promotion and the championship were eventually secured against Airdrie in the second to last game, with Andy clinching victory with a last minute penalty to make the score 3-1.

Despite Morton's fine performance in winning the First Division championship in 1978, the doubters were still writing them off for their debut Premier League season. Initially they did struggle, but soon found their feet. Morton fans could certainly be forgiven a certain smugness as the season dawned. They knew exactly what was to be unleashed on the unsuspecting Premier League. Andy gave warning of his intentions for the Premier League in a pre-season friendly at home to Watford. A 40 yard howitzer of a free kick just about uprooted the goal on its way into the net.

The match was probably the start of Andy's 'goalden' era, when he was scoring goals that no one else could. He was trying things that no other player even thought about, and they were coming off. Long-range shots and free kicks were flying in from all angles, and suddenly the Scottish press realised that they had a star in their midst. Unfortunately it was too late for the Scottish national side, who had suffered in the World Cup at the hands - or should it be the feet - of Peru's version of Ritchie, Teofilo Cubillas. Scotland goalie Alan Rough had stood rooted to the spot as Cubillas rifled two rockets past him in 1978.

It was good preparation for Roughie as Andy would do it to him on a regular basis in the Premier League. But according to Andy he could have been in Argentina with Roughie.

Ally McLeod wanted to take me to Argentina but the SFA

committee said it wouldn't look good taking a part-time player. He said he wanted me in the squad although he wouldn't use me all the time, but I was ready for international football.

Morton's first season in the Premier League was an unqualified success, and despite the all-round excellence of Benny Rooney's side, there can be no argument that Andy Ritchie's goals and the all-round play were the dominant factors in keeping 'Ton in the Premier League in that first season. Andy was the League's top scorer with a string of sensational efforts. At the end of the season, although new Scotland manager Jock Stein could ignore him, no one else could and Andy walked away with the Football Writers' player of the year award for 1979.

Celebrated football writer Hugh Taylor said at the time: 'His outrageous gifts border on genius'. Andy is refreshingly candid and modest about what he was such a sensation.

The whole country had endured a horrendous World Cup in Argentina. Football in Scotland needed a lift, and I was there in the right place at the right time. The press had to find something different to write about. Something that was new and fresh, and that was when it all started for me.

There were still those who doubted him though.

It was always as if both myself and Morton always had to go that extra mile to prove ourselves. With Morton it was, 'Well they've done well to get in the promotion race, but Hearts and Dundee will sort them out'. Then it was 'well they've done well to win promotion, but the big boys will sort them out'. And so it went on, but we consistently proved the doubters wrong. We had great spirit. And it was the same with me. I constantly had to prove myself. And then the press built this persona of me, the idle idol thing, and it just grew arms and legs.

Andy came to the fore just when work-rate began to out-distance talent in many supposedly knowledgeable football people's minds. Just as his compatriots south of the border, like Stan Bowles, Rodney Marsh and Frank Worthington, were being usurped by 'team players' who took the man first and asked questions later, Andy too suffered from his supposed laziness.

I can't deny I loved the adulation, and my first few years at Morton were fantastic, but I wanted international football, and that meant full-time football. Morton made noises about it, but it never happened and looking back that was a mistake, although we achieved a hell of a lot with what we had. So, I was constantly looking for a move. When I joined Morton I looked on it as taking a step back to take two steps forward, and all I was looking for was a move I had been promised when I joined.

So Andy was constantly badgering Morton for a move but a combination of his image and Morton looking for too much money denied Andy the transfer he craved. Bids were certainly made for him. Hearts bid £200,000 as did Sheffield Wednesday, managed by Jack Charlton. Liverpool enquired but were put off by Morton's asking price.

Andy was at the peak of his powers in 1979 as Morton powered to the top of the Premier League. He was the finest attacker in the country, the only player apart from Dalglish who could rival the best of the Continentals, yet he couldn't get a look in. Stein compromised slightly, and capped Andy once for the Scottish League and as an overage player in the Under-21's. Andy scored in the League match but was never to get the call for the full national side. Morton's second season in the Premier League provided many highs and lows and more memorable Ritchie moments. One of the disappointments was the League Cup semi-final defeat against Aberdeen. Morton had already beaten the Dons twice that season, and should have gone into the match full of confidence, but some of the players froze and Morton lost 2-1. Andy still feels the disappointment keenly.

We really should have beaten Aberdeen that day. It was probably one of the few times that as a team we didn't do ourselves justice. Aberdeen got let off the hook that day and they knew it. The game was over before we started to play.

In Morton's third season in the Premier League they reached

the Scottish Cup semi-final, a match that would provide a defining moment in Andy's career.

The 1981 cup run provided Andy's finest and worst memories of his time at Cappielow. He had scored a wonder goal against Aberdeen in the fourth round, and Morton faced Rangers in the semi-final. Benny Rooney didn't make too many mistakes as Morton boss, but his decision to leave Andy on the bench that day was a costly one for Morton. Benny afterwards explained his decision.

It was one of the hardest decisions that I ever had to make in football. It's easy to say in hindsight that I should have played Andy, but I knew it would be a physical match, and decided to bring in a different type of player to Andy, and after all, Rangers left out Davie Cooper. But I made the decision at the time, and you live or die by it.

Andy himself claims that Benny Rooney never gave that reason to him, saying merely that he had decided to leave him out of the starting XI.

To be honest I wasn't playing well. I was playing well in the cup, but I was struggling for consistency in the league. When Benny told me on the Friday that he was putting me on the bench, I thought he was kidding. I remember thinking that he would phone me on the Friday night and tell me he had changed his mind. I didn't take it too well at the time. If Benny had given me a valid reason at the time, like I wasn't playing well, or it was tactical, it would have been easier to take. But he never really gave me a valid reason. He said afterwards that he didn't really want to leave me out and that was why he couldn't answer me at that time.

In the event Rooney was proven right about the physical side of the match, which wasn't helped by inconsistent refereeing. Morton were not a particularly physical side. Morton had their usual goal disallowed and lost the match 2-1, and had two players ordered off. Andy came off the bench, almost inevitably scoring with a penalty, but it was too late to make a real difference. Morton had blown a great chance to reach their first Scottish Cup final in 33 years.

Looking back on it, it wasn't like the semi against Aberdeen when we went cold and froze a bit. We had gained experience to win matches like that so obviously it was a huge disappointment. I know I had let Benny down at times, but I felt he let me down that day. Unfortunately I wasn't mature enough to accept it and get on with it.

The side began to break up shortly afterwards, with Jim Tolmie, Neil Orr and Bobby Thomson all moving on. It was always felt the big man would follow them out of the door. He had actually first asked for a move on the eve of Morton's first season in the Premier League.

Whenever a player left Morton for a bigger club, nobody resented it, because we were all only too delighted for them. Because of the spirit in the dressing room we never thought why him and not me? After all, we're all in the game to better ourselves and play at as high a level as possible.

Somehow the move never materialised and Andy's form suffered. Disillusionment set in when it became evident that no big club was prepared to spend big money on a player who wasn't willing to conform to the accepted practice of drowning in his own sweat. Two more undistinguished seasons followed. He had averaged 27 goals a season in his first four seasons at Cappielow, but that had fallen to 11 by 1982. In his last season at Morton Andy only started 16 League games, and Morton were relegated. Andy admits now that he was disillusioned, but didn't have the wherewithal to do anything about it.

The game came too easy for me, and that's why I only played till I was 27. The game just happened for me; if it didn't happen a lot of times I didn't know why. When I ran into a bad spell I didn't know how to make it better. Guys like Jim Holmes did. They worked harder, they knuckled down. That's why they had long careers. I didn't do that. And that's to my detriment.

Team mate Jim Holmes says: 'If Andy had left Morton earlier when he was at his peak, he would have played much longer. But Morton held on and held on'. Andy agrees:

By the time I got to the end of my spell there I had lost the eye for the game, and needed to move on. That was what had been promised to me when I joined, but it should have happened sooner. I had taken my eye off the ball. I needed full-time training for a start. I wasn't receiving incoming phone calls. You could put it that way.

But when Andy finally did leave Morton it was for a similar sized club, Motherwell, the club he had supported as a boy. The legendary Jock Wallace signed him, and Andy tried hard to get himself fit, and actually got on very well with the ex-Rangers manager. 'Big Jock got me fit but wouldn't let me play. If I spent more than a couple of seconds on the ball he'd be screaming at me to get rid of it'.

Then Bobby Watson took over from Wallace and after 13 games and four goals, Andy moved again. He had brief spells with Clydebank and East Stirling, but by now he had let his fitness go. He moved on to Albion Rovers, and began season 1984-85 as player coach. By this time, however, Andy knew the game was up, and after only three games he quit. Totally disenchanted with football, he had accepted a job outside football in London, and one of the greatest talents ever seen in Scottish football was lost to the game at the age of 28. In the 20 years since he retired, Andy has returned frequently to the game he graced, but never as a player. He has been assistant manager at Hamilton, and coached at St Mirren and Celtic youngsters. But possibly his greatest enjoyment has been in his role as talent spotter. He has travelled all over Europe in his capacity as chief scout for a number of clubs including Derby and Aston Villa. And of course it was while working in that role for Celtic that he helped bring Paul Lambert and Pierre Van Hooijdonk to the club. Now older and wiser, Andy knows he made mistakes.

Where does one start to pick the best of Andy's goals? Was it the long range rocket against Watford, or the free kick that was shown all around Britain against the hapless Rough? Andy lined Roughie's wall up for him, then cheekily peeked round it before placing the ball in the top corner of the net. Or perhaps it was when he did what Pele couldn't do and scored from the halfway line against Dundee United, or maybe it was the one that didn't stand against Celtic at Parkhead when he powered home a 30 yarder into the teeth of a gale. Andy's own favourite is when he chipped giant Rangers keeper Peter McCloy.

One of the really frustrating things about Andy's career is that so little of it is captured for posterity. Andy played in the days before saturated television coverage, and the television companies tended to show Rangers or Celtic every week. Consequently, only a couple of Andy's wonderful goals are available to view. Thankfully, one goal that was recorded is perhaps his greatest. Morton against Aberdeen, Scottish fourth round, February 1981. The big man wasn't having the best of seasons, but he reminded us all of his genius that day. Morton were Aberdeen's bogey team at the time. Under Alex Ferguson the Dons were just beginning to dominate Scottish football. They were reigning champions, and feared no one, except Morton who had beaten them several times in the preceding few seasons. As Alex McLeish freely admits, they, and particularly goalkeeper Jim Leighton, were terrified of Andy. This was evident when, after about 20 minutes of the match, Andy received the ball with his back to the Aberdeen goal 20 yards out. Behind him, defending deep, were left back Doug Considine, McLeish, Willie Miller and Leighton, in other words three-fifths of what was soon to be Scotland's defence. The pass was really no more than a hopeful punt from John Marr, but Andy took the ball on his chest and clicked the ball up and over his head. As he pivoted Considine performed a fair impersonation of a rubber man and slipped, probably out of terror, and McLeish and Miller tried to close Andy down. On the face of it, it was text book defending by the Scotland central defenders, but in reality their faces were transfixed like a pair of rabbits caught in the glare of car headlights. Leighton hopped about like a toothless, bandy-legged cat on hot bricks. Completely unfazed, Andy controlled the ball on the turn and curved the ball with the outside of his right boot around the two defenders and past Leighton into the only uncovered area of the goal. Cappielow erupted. It was a special goal even by Andy's standards. It was the only goal of the match. To put the goal in perspective, Aberdeen did not lose another Scottish Cup match until 1985. After that match they won the cup for three years in a row, probably because they managed to avoid Morton! Andy regularly gave Rough and Leighton nightmares with his shooting accuracy. Probably the game that started it all was in Morton's first season in the Premier League in a match at Cappielow, when Andy curled a free kick past Leighton from way out on the left touchline. From then on it became a regular occurrence.

Mark McGhee remembers the effect Andy had on his old mentor at Aberdeen, Alex Ferguson. 'Big Andy worried the life out of Fergie, especially at dead balls. In all my career I think only Glenn Hoddle and Manny Kaltz rival Andy as an accomplished striker of the ball'.

It goes without saying that Andy enjoyed an incredible rapport with the Morton fans. His humour was legendary. He often took time out for a wisecrack, and to call him an entertainer is an understatement. The Morton fans adored him, and still do. In a recent poll Andy was overwhelmingly voted the greatest-ever Morton player. There's no doubt that if he had been playing today, Andy would be a superstar. In a business where David Beckham has become one of the most famous men on the planet, and made untold millions through his talents, what price Andy Ritchie? What price genius? Andy, thanks for the memories.

Alex McLeish (Aberdeen & Scotland)

Alex McLeish graced the fields of Pittordrie more than 500 times, scoring 25 goals in a glittering career. He was capped by his country on 77 occasions and he is a Scotland Hall of Fame inductee.

In November 2007 as manager of the national team Scotland stood top of their group having beaten Italy and France. A win at home to Italy would see the Tartan Army booking their place at Euro 2008 whilst their neighbours south of the border would struggle. Sadly Scotland lost with the last kick of the match and none of the home countries would appear in the finals.

Of Andy Ritchie these comments are attributed to the Scottish manager:

"Big Andy was always full of verbal - always had a smile on his face especially when he nutmegged you. I think in fact with the goal he scored in the Scottish, players were always so terrified of Andy nutmegging them that they would shut their legs and he curled it roon them, you know. He had such a good footballing brain that he sussed things like that. He scored one from 50 yards and he was in his own half, nobody near him and he shouted 'Big Yin, ye'd better pick me up, I'll probably score from here - you're talking 60-70 yards and I was thinking, he's got a point, I better get across. He was the scourge of the Dons in those days.

"Andy Ritchie scored from the halfway line once. Jim Leighton was absolutely terrified of Andy. It was his worst nightmare. Jim used to pray and hope Andy wasn't playing - I think we all did to be honest. Big Jim would go through the team sheet - 1,2,3,…11 Ritchie - oh no! We actually put Jim's understudy, John Gardiner, in goal, for a cup tie at Cappielow and because this boy didn't have the same fear as Jim he played a blinder and we won 2-1. Andy had one of those ones, on the 18 yard line - a free kick which he usually scored. He curled it round the wall and the big fellow made a great save." (Alex McLeish, quoted in Vincent P. Gillen, *Greenock Morton 1874-1999*)

"Morton seemed to raise their game for us even more than when Rangers or Celtic went to Cappielow. But before a cup tie Alex (Sir Alex Ferguson) was really nervous but I honestly couldn't see us losing it - but Andy Ritchie scored a wonder goal again, the outside of the right peg, curling it round three defenders into the top corner. After we got beaten Fergie just sat up the bus in a huff … didn't talk to us and anybody that smiled was fined a tenner. 'If I hear any laughing up the back of that f...... bus I'll fine you a tenner - anybody smiles - fiver'.

"It didn't seem to matter who Benny brought into the team either. I played against a succession of strikers, including Andy Ritchie. Benny could have probably played himself and Mike Jackson and they would have still beat us - we just could not win down at Cappielow."

I wrote to Alex McLeish in November 2007 shortly before the Italy game, his last as coach before the much publicised move to Premiership side Birmingham City. Alex's impact was immediate when City beat Spurs in his first match in charge at White Hart Lane. Alex responded to my letter and this is the full extract from the Scotland manager, as he was at the time:

"No doubt about it, Big Andy seemed to have something against Aberdeen FC. He earned his player of the year award because of his performances against us!!

We tried every tactic to stop him and you have to hold your hands up and say that sometimes he was unplayable. It wasn't that he dominated for 90 minutes, it was more the odd flash of genius that, quite a few times, was enough to clinch victory. Andy, in alliance with his resilient and tough team mates, were a team who gave a great Aberdeen side more problems than any other Scottish team."

Mr McLeish even sent me a signed photograph to use in this book.

Stewart McCartney mine host at The Spinnaker Hotel, Gourock:
"Andy Ritchie was simply the best player I have ever seen at Cappielow Park. He is always welcome here!"

Craig Brown CBE (Rangers, Dundee, Falkirk & Scotland):
Craig Brown was an educated player who played at the top, winning a League Championship medal with Dundee before in

later life becoming manager of the national team. Craig is a qualified schoolteacher and is currently working as Director of Football at Derby County in the English Premier League. He was the first man to spot Andy Ritchie's potential.

"I must have had a charmed life as a teacher because when I went to Bellshill, to Belvedere School, I had enthusiastic support from the head teacher and the rest of the staff. We excelled in football, swimming and gymnastics and had some great individuals. One of my pupils at that primary school was not only in my football team but also in the class of which I was appointed teacher. He went on to become a top player and in 1979 was named Scottish Footballer of the Year. You know him as Andy Ritchie, and his career spanned Celtic, Greenock Morton and eventually Motherwell. He was impressive even as a boy - a very big lad who was obviously destined for an exciting career in football.

"Andy Ritchie was a prime example of the argument against eleven-a-side football on big pitches for kids. All Andy had to do was get into the opponent's half and shoot. Because of his size, and the size of the goalmouth when compared to the lack of size of the goalkeeper, he would grab a handful of goals every time he played. You could get a jumbo jet to fly under the crossbar and over the young goalkeeper's head, and Andy soon learned where to place his shot. He was a prized asset to us because he could score so easily, but because his size and ability gave him such an advantage over other boys of his own age, he effectively ruined the game each time he played. It wasn't his fault, but it did show how inappropriate it was to have eleven-a-side matches in that primary age group. I tried to even the games a little by making arbitrary rules such as he could only score with his head one day, or from outside the area in another. It succeeded in evening up the games and hopefully furthered his football education too." (Craig Brown, *The Game of My Life*, Blake Publishing, 2001)

Billy Thomson, Morton fan
"My son Stuart was aged 9 when he met his idol, Andy

Ritchie.

"The photograph was featured in *Top Soccer Magazine* on 22nd December 1979. A week later when Morton were playing St Mirren at Paisley, big Andy saw Stuart standing at the corner flag with me. He said to Stuart, 'How you doing wee man. Do you want to see me scoring a goal direct from a corner kick?'

"Guess what? He did.

"He just turned around and gave one of his big toothless grins, winked at Stuart and Andy added, 'I told you so didn't I?'"

Jim Sinclair, match photographer & Morton supporter

"I did not know anyone who could bend a ball like 'sugar'. I can't remember how many times he would step up to take a corner kick, usually if I recall from the right hand corner. He would hit the ball and before anyone had moved it was in the back of the net, keeper beaten and the crowd on their feet with joy.

"I can remember the cheers which still ring in my ears to this day, when Andy would be brought on from the subs bench, 'the Ton' would be down a goal or only drawing, Andy was the hero that was going to save the day, and often he did.

"I feel privileged that not only was I there to capture some of his great moments, but that I was able to see and enjoy his skills as a true Morton supporter. The man is truly a legend."

Benny Rooney, Celtic, Dundee United & Partick Thistle & Manager of Greenock Morton FC 1976-83

Andy Ritchie played under Benny in what many people regard as the glory days and possibly made more comments about his player than most others. Benny has retired from the game he graced and is now mine host at the Queens Park Café in Glasgow, a café that incidentally sells more than just coffee!

"We signed Andy through the goalkeeping situation. Celtic wanted Roy Baines and I knew all about Andy. I knew what I was taking on, but I knew what he could give us. Roy was a good keeper but I felt I could always replace him. The deal went through without a hitch. Andy came in and just started being Andy and he quickly gelled with Mark McGhee.

"One of my biggest regrets was in the semi-final of the cup leaving Andy out, … it might have been a mistake at the time but I felt against Ranger, I mean they left Cooper out as well, showed what kind of game it was going to be." (Benny Rooney, quoted in Vincent P. Gillen, *Greenock Morton 1874-1999*)

"There had been a lot of hype before the game about it being a physical match and in the event that's how it turned out. In hindsight you could say I should have played big Andy from the start. [Fearing a physical match, Benny controversially left star man Andy Ritchie on the bench.] We got too involved in the physical stuff and, after letting a lot go in the first half, the referee came down on us in the second half. But looking back on it now, a few players did lose their head a bit and that's what cost us the game." [Morton lost 2-1!] (Benny Rooney, quoted in Graeme Ross, *More Morton Greats*, Breedon Books, 2005)

Benny goes on:
"Ritchie came at the right time - he was the cream at the top of the cake at the time … he got the label of being a lazy player and he nurtured that a little bit … I used to train him on his own, he trained hard. He was a character, his skills were unbelievable, his passing, his vision, dead ball situations … there was a free kick at a pre-season game, we had a wee thing with Watford, who were progressing at the time, Taylor was the manager and they came about three seasons in a row. I can always remember this one game, Andy had a free kick just over the centre circle … they don't put up a wall or any thing and Mick (Jackson) says, it was his first game, 'He's not going to shoot from there'. 'Just leave him,' I says. He hits the ball in the roof of the net … he was that good." (Benny Rooney, quoted in Vincent P. Gillen, *Greenock Morton 1874-1999*)

"The time I miss is when I get together with football people. When I look back at some of the players we had at Morton. Andy Ritchie Player of the Year. Jim Duffy Player of the Year. I look back with pride and joy. I get a number of Morton fans who still write to me. That means a lot to me. I've said it time and time again that the best years of my entire career were at Morton." (Benny Rooney, quoted in Graeme Ross, *More Morton Greats*)

"I remember watching him play for Morton. He had the God-given talent to make the ball do all the work and ping passes round the pitch regularly. There are many players who can do this maybe once or twice in a game, but Andy did it ninety per cent of the game. He always joked that it saved him running. He was also the very first free kick specialist I ever saw. I am convinced that some Brazilian saw him and thought, 'I'll try that too'. There are few genuine stand-out one-offs in life. Andy is one of that few. Morton fans worshipped him and with good reason. He was for them what Jimmy Johnstone and Jim Baxter were to old firm fans."

Mike Jackson (Celtic & Queen of the South & assistant manager to Rooney at Morton)
Benny Rooney signed Mike as part of his backroom staff. "Mike was great for me and the club. It was a great partnership."

The comments attributed to Mike about Andy Ritchie are well documented in the various publications. They include:

"Hal (Stewart) was brilliant for Scottish football … he had vision way beyond his years but he had this reputation as a super salesman … top dog … he could sell snow to Eskimos … great patter, character but as soon as someone was brought into the team Hal was rubbing his hands … 'I'll get a million for him' (obvious reference to Ritchie). We kept saying to him 'You're not working for the Co-operative, this is Morton we are talking about'.

"The players were great with Andy … I couldn't have

handled him as a player, I'd have been fighting with him, because to be honest he did f... all at times. I'd sit in the dugout and say, 'get him off'. It was the funniest thing ... after a couple of months Benny ... Christ we used to argue in that dugout, 'get him off' and Benny would say 'no he might do something, he might score'. About six weeks later Benny would say to me 'get the boards out, get him off!' and then I went 'hold on a mo ... he might score!' You suffered him (Andy), and I say that in the best possible way because he's a lovely big guy. You took him off and he would sit beside you on the bench ... I used to smoke and he'd say 'quick, Benny's not looking, gies a fag'. You could never get angry with him.

"He got a reputation for being idle Andy but in actual fact, when we did sprints ... we used to have bets ... the big b......, you ought to have seen him run. If you said to him, 'up and down the park' and put a few quid at stake Big Andy would be hard to beat.

"Without his goals we wouldn't have stayed in the Premier League, but at the same token, he's got to thank a lot of other people because the spade work they did for him was unbelievable. Because the boys got on so well together, they accepted Andy's failings, because everybody has different abilities. They were willing to muck in a bit harder because Andy was the icing on the cake. He would pull a goal out of nowhere for you. The boys realised that."

Mrs Elizabeth (Bessie) Ritchie, Andy's mam
Bessie Ritchie has many anecdotes about her son's life. The best two are thought to be:

"I was on the railway station at Uddingston (the home of Tunnock's Caramel Wafers and the birthplace of the late, great Jimmy 'Jinky' Johnstone) waiting for me train. On the platform was a young man who looked absolutely frozen. As we were the only two people on that bleak day we struck up a conversation, as you do, passing the time of day. In the course of our wee chat the young man said he was from Greenock.

I replied, 'Oh my son played for Greenock,' and left it at that.

A little later he asked, 'What was your son's name?' and I replied, 'Andy Ritchie'.

The look on his face was a picture.

'You are Andy Ritchie's mum?' he asked.

I nodded.

'My dad used to take me to see Andy at Cappielow. He was the greatest player I have ever seen,' he enthused.

I think it made his day.

My only regret was that I wasn't wearing my best coat."

And a little gem from Cappielow:

"I didn't see Andrew play that often. [Bessie always calls her son Andrew. When Andy is annoyed with his mam, he calls her Elizabeth!] I didn't like to see him get hurt and I didn't want him heading the ball. [She need not have worried on that score.]

"On one occasion I was at Cappielow and Andy was left on the ground injured after a crunching tackle. As he lay on the muddy pitch some of the fans began to sing, 'Andy wants his mummy, Andy wants his mummy.'

"I was surprised and turned to my friend and said, 'I wonder how they know I am at the game.' That provoked smiles all round as it was a popular chant in those days for any player who the crowd felt was not really injured.

"Nobody knew 'Andy's mummy' was in fact at the game."

Ian Archer, Morton fan and football writer
"Mike Jackson shook Andy's wet jersey as he came off the field. 'Don't tell me you've been sweating?'

"'Naw,' said the Footballer of the Year - 'I fell in a puddle.'"

Ian Archer called Andy Ritchie "the greatest entertainer we've got … the sharpest finisher in the country as well. Dundee United did a silly thing, taking the lead and rousing Ritchie from his slumber. Half a dozen Ritches in Scottish football would make Hampden Park too tiny to hold the fans wanting to see them."

Vincent P. Gillen, author and Morton fan

Vincent works at the McLean Museum and Art Gallery in Kelly Street, Greenock. The McLean is one of the best municipal museums in Scotland with displays on local history, James Watt, ship engine models, natural history exhibits and an excellent fine art collection.

Vincent is the author of a comprehensive history on Greenock Morton, *Greenock Morton 1874-1999*, which is on sale in the museum shop.

I met Vincent in December 2007 and received his authority to include references from his book in *The King of Cappielow*. He writes:

"I remember at Hal Stewart's testimonial he scored against Alan Rough direct from a corner. The funny thing was he had done it against Rough the previous week in a League game and everyone was shouting at Rough that he would do it again - sure enough! He even helped Rough line up the wall!"

Jim MacVicar
Trust Member and Albert Hotel Morton supporter

"I started my love affair with Greenock Morton FC as a 8 or 9 year old when Andy Ritchie came to Cappielow. I certainly have a few memories of Andy at Cappielow and he remains my all-time favourite. In my eyes the most gifted player ever to pull on a Morton shirt. I also have my 1st Morton strip from back in the late 70s (the type you see Andy in) which is signed by 'god' himself."

Chick Young, BBC football correspondent for Scotland

Chick is captain of the legendary charity football team Dukla Pumpherston. The name Dukla Pumpherston was coined by Tony Roper, the Scottish comedian who starred with Rab C. Nesbitt. Andy Ritchie and Tony are founder members of the team. Chick has written many words about Andy over the years, some of which have been described as 'caustic'. But you judge for yourselves:

"Hal once told Andy Ritchie to pack a bag because he was

going away for the weekend. Andy thought Hal had sent him up with Manchester United or something. They arrived at Stobbo Castle health farm - he said lose a stone - 'I'll see you in a week'.

"Andy Ritchie - I can close my eyes and see the day as clear as you like. Morton were getting a doing by Dundee United and the defence was under siege. Big Andy was standing in the centre circle, hands inside his shirt sleeves, looking at the seagulls, bored out of his skull, when Davie Hayes blootered this ball out - it was just Andy and David Hegarty left, and Andy, you couldn't slip a copy of the *Greenock Telegraph* under his feet when he jumped. Hegarty jumped and missed and Ritchie did what Pele couldn't do and volleyed the ball past Hamish from the halfway line! Andy was the epitome of the Scottish footballer - fat, lazy bastard but with great ball skill.

"But, in the case of Greenock Morton, I talk not just with the wallet but with the heart.

"I have had a special affection for them since the early sixties, when the late Haldane Stewart, one of the most remarkable men I ever met in football, breathed life into the club.

"At that time, they were in much the same mess as now, but Hal - the Arthur Daley of Scottish football - applied his showman approach with a little bit of wheeling and dealing and dragged them out of the gutter.

"In fact, Morton were so successful that they topped the Premier Division at the end of the year and the great man proudly told the players they had a choice of Christmas bonus.

"They could have a turkey or a pair of jeans! All stored, presumably, in a lock-up somewhere.

"I loved that man, I really did. And, with Benny Rooney and Mike Jackson in charge of a team led by the Ambling Alp, big Andy Ritchie, alongside Bobby 'the Beast' Russell, Davie 'Hannibal' Hayes and the rest, Morton were the Crazy Gang of the day." (*BBC Sport*)

John Mullin, journalist and Morton fan

"It was the Idle Idol of Cappielow Park who first attracted me to Morton. (Yes it was a clinical decision, rather than one forced on me by birth.) Years after Ritchie had quit playing, criminally at the age of 27, I was sustained by the moments of his footballing beauty; the humbling of Alan Rough (not difficult in itself, but impressive in its regularity); the strike from his own half into the wind against Celtic, at Parkhead, disallowed because John McNeil was standing in an offside position away out at the corner flag; and the most sublime moment of all; the 20th minute winner against Aberdeen in the Scottish Cup on St Valentine's Day, 1981. I have it on video and anyone is welcome to see it.

"Ritchie was simply the best player I have ever seen; more than 6ft tall, at times ballooning to 16 stone, but with the best balance, ball control, passing ability and shooting power ever combined in a Scottish player. He was fat and slow, his work rate hardly dynamic, but there was no one like him.

"And he was named Scottish Footballer of the Year in 1979 - the first player from a wee club ever to wear the crown.

"Ritchie should have become an entry in the dictionary - a verb seldom with an object; a very complex idea meaning at once great and gormless, jumping without leaving the ground (rather like a tin of salmon), disappearing from the surface of the earth for long periods in a match, and then returning from nowhere to score a goal of sublime skill.

"Some people can quote Shakespeare, the war poets, even all the lyrics to *Band on the Run*. [*Band on the Run* is an album by Wings, released in 1973. It was 1974's top-selling album, and revitalised Paul McCartney's critical standing.]

"I can only recite this, nicked from William Hunter's 1983 Morton versus Motherwell match report in the then *Glasgow Herald*: 'towards the interval he scored a goal the likes of which will not be seen again until he himself does it again. He was standing at the far corner of the box. He looked as if he had just come out for a stroll and to admire the grass. He then just hit the ball. He didn't seem to move but just hit the ball.

To the east and south it bent through the air by four or five yards. That may not be possible but that was how it looked from the centre of the stand. Hugh Sproat in the Motherwell goal did not move to the left, nor did he move to the right. He appeared mesmerised. The ball screamed past him into the corner of the net.'

"Ritchie's big money transfer never came - apparently £5,000 was all that separated him from a move to Liverpool - and he was out of the game at 27 … Ritchie never got his chance for Scotland. When he scored a hat-trick against Dundee United a few days before the selection of a Scotland squad for a European Championship qualifier, the crowd started screaming 'Ritchie for Scotland'. But he had a history with Jock Stein, the then Scotland manager. Stein had offloaded Ritchie from Celtic to Morton after Ritchie disobeyed the manager's screamed instructions from the dugout. He had put the ball down for a free kick, blasted it home from miles out, and then treated Mr Stein to a two-fingered salute. [See Andy's response in the exclusive interview.]

"The Scotland manager prevaricated when tackled about Ritchie's possible inclusion that Sunday on Scotsport." (*Guardian Weekend*, 14th June 1997)

Arthur Montford, anchorman extraordinaire, had no doubts with regard to the latter, however. The titles ended with "Goals from what must be Scotland's new strike force: Kenny Dalglish of Liverpool and Andy Ritchie of Morton".

Stein relented and Ritchie was named in the Under-21 squad as an over-age player.

In December 2007, Gillian Donaldson, the Chief Executive at Morton, arranged for me to meet Mr Montford at half-time in the 2-2 draw with Livingston. Arthur is to Scottish football what David Coleman, Kenneth Wolstenholme and John 'Mottie' Motson is to English fans.

But he is a legend!

It was indeed a pleasure to meet such a great man in the twilight of his years and still supporting Morton Football

Club.

Ronnie Miller, policeman and Morton fan

Ronnie Miller tells what it was like working at Cappielow as a policeman. An avid Morton fan, he recalls the day Morton went top of the Premier League in December 1979:

"I was right behind the Sinclair St goal and my pal was under the scoreboard, I got dogs abuse every time I passed. Anyway they got a free kick, of course the rules were, they still are, that you're there to watch the crowd not the game but I couldn't help it, I kept turning round - they got a free kick, I couldn't miss Ritchie taking a free kick and then of course the Celtic keeper and defence are waiting for the usual curl around the wall. Instead he put it down the side to John McNeil who crossed it in low to Bobby Thomson who knocked it in. The ball just about landed at my feet and I couldn't contain myself." (*Greenock Morton 1874-1999*)

Andrew M. Cubie, football supporter

"The first football game that you ever attend can influence you for life; as a parent it's important to get it right when you first take the kids. A dull turgid game will put the children off for life; so might an easy romp. You want them thrilled, excited and above all engaged.

"After much pleading to see a 'live' game, I took my boys aged 7 and 5 to see Scotland under 21's vs Belgium in the 1998 qualifier for Euro 2000. The main attraction was Mark Burchill, a young Celtic player making a name for himself.

"Half-time and the queue for pies, my younger son waited patiently then couldn't reach the hatch. Helpful fans lifted him up; appetite satisfied, and Andy Ritchie was there.

"Possibly the most talented Scottish footballer ever, who lit up the late 70's and the early 80's for Morton. He combined the skills of Pele and Maradona with the energy of a hibernating bear. Andy looked as if he'd been in the pie queue that night, several times in fact, but still attracted real attention as he was so fondly remembered."

Allan McGraw, Hibernian & Greenock Morton

Allan McGraw had an association with Morton FC that was to last 36 years. He is known as 'Mr Morton' but supports a Glasgow club as he actually comes from Govan. Labelled 'the nicest man in Scottish football', he scored 58 goals in the 1963-64 season so he knows all about hitting the back of the net. He played for Hibs as well as being a Morton legend. It was his penalty that took Morton to the 1963 League Cup final.

"Andy didn't realise how much people held him in awe, especially young kids. He couldn't understand why they all worshipped him, what hold he had on them.

"Jimmy Miller ran up the field and gave the ball to Andy and then went to the by-line waiting for the ball back. Andy tried to sell the guy a dummy, but whether he was too clever or never bought it, the fella blocked him and got the ball, Andy shouted to Jimmy, 'Jimmy, Get him!' but Jimmy was away on the by-line, but that's Andy for you.

"I remember watching the scout from Manchester City who was up watching Andy. I got Andy afterwards and said the scout was watching, that he could go places and Andy said, 'Ah, I'm no changing'."

Peter Livingstone, football writer

"Andy Ritchie orchestrated our midfield with subtle promptings and precise passes. Needing a win against Airdrie and having been dragged back to 1-1 by a rare Davie Hayes goal, there were just five minutes left when in true comic book style - crash, bang, wallop, Russell had put Goldthorpe through to sweetly lob the ball into the goal. Then down went Goldthorpe and Ritchie gleefully struck home the penalty. It was 3-1 and 'We were the Champions." (*Greenock Morton 1874-1999*)

Roy Dyer, fan now living in Australia

"My favourite memory was promotion to the Premier League and dancing in the fountain in the town in front of the library.

I want to thank the people at the club; in a pretty unhappy childhood (for all the reasons that have afflicted Greenock) these were some of the happiest days of my childhood." (*Greenock Morton 1874-1999*)

Jim McLean, Hamilton, Clyde, Kilmarnock and Dundee United

Jim McLean's career playing football spanned 25 years and he was manager of Dundee United for 22 years. He may best remembered by fans as the manager who took an average club at the time with no major silverware and little European experience to a UEFA Cup final. He took Dundee United to ten domestic Cup finals and the Scottish League title.

"You never like to get beaten, but when you lose to class like Ritchie's, it makes it much easier to take. The first goal was a fluke, the second was a penalty and the third was one of the best goals I've ever seen."

That hat-trick prompted the crowd to chant, "'Ritchie for Scotland, Ritchie for Scotland". Unfortunately that was an ambition Andy only achieved as an over-age player with the Under-21 squad, despite pressure from the Scottish Football Association.

Roger Graham, Sports Editor, *Greenock Telegraph*

"The surprising thing about this last goal was that Ritchie won a tackle first, to set up the goal."

In an interview with Ian Archer after scoring the hat-trick in the 4-1 win over Dundee United, Andy explained his third goal, a screamer of a 30-yard free kick.

"I'd been fouled and was having a rest. The referee wanted me to get up and carry on. I said to him 'Mr Anderson, I'll get up, I'll take the free kick and put it in the top corner of the net. If I do that will you knock five minutes off the end of the game so I can get away early? I kept my end of the bargain. Unfortunately Mr Anderson didn't keep his. We had to play the full 90 minutes."

Exclusive Interview with Andy Ritchie

Andy Ritchie and I finally met on 26th October 2007 in the Spinnaker Hotel, Albert Road, Gourock, where we enjoyed lunch together. This is my account of that interview, verified later by Andy.

After asking Andy the usual questions about his childhood, parents and brothers and sister to support my research for this book, I asked a series of questions that supporters of Morton, Celtic and other clubs have been asking for years.

Q. You were the first student to graduate from the Celtic Boys Club but who actually first spotted the raw talent you had?
A. *John Dempsey, whose son played for Hamilton, although Craig Brown, who was my teacher at Belvedere, says in his book he spotted me as well.*

Q. You had trials with Manchester United, Coventry, Everton, Middlesbrough, Rangers and Celtic, so why did you choose Celtic?
A. *I went for a trial at Middlesbrough when Stan Anderson and Harold Shepherdson were there. I even went and spent a Christmas on Teesside. That's ironic really, because many years later I was involved in the transfer of Bernie Slaven from Albion Rovers to Boro, where he would become a legend. But I trained with Rangers on a Thursday night and Celtic on a Tuesday. I chose Celtic because I liked their youth team coach, Wally Fernie.*

Q. It is alleged that you didn't get on with Jock Stein and that you didn't always do what you were told. It is said that on one occasion you ignored his instructions, smashed the ball home from 30 yards and then gave him a two-fingered salute. Is that true?

A. *It is not true that I gave the two-fingered salute to Jock Stein. That is a myth. What I did do was wave and smile after I planted the ball in the net. I got some advice from Jock at the time. The big man said, "If you take the cotton wool out of your ears and put it in your mouth, you will do a lot better." I still remember those words today.*

Q. In all that time, even though he offloaded you to Morton, there is no record that you ever bad-mouthed the great man. That must have been difficult when after you scored a hat-trick against Dundee United for The Ton the crowd responded by chanting "Ritchie for Scotland".

A. Andy smiled (and later in our interview expanded on his thoughts about never having played for Scotland at full international level). *Yes it hurt!*

Q. I understand the Scottish FA intervened and made Stein take you to the next Scotland game?

A. *Pressure was applied after the Dundee United game and I was included in the squad prior to a Euro Qualifier. So the simple answer is YES he was forced to include me.*

Q. But still, once out of the country, he didn't play you in the first team. He gave you a place as the over-age player with the Under-21s. How did he explain that and how did you feel?

A. *Two days before the game he came to my room and told me I wasn't playing in the team. He said he had selected me as an over-age player in the Under-21 team.*

I was angry, disappointed - naturally. But what could I do?

"Sorry Andy, I ask the questions!"

Q. So you played in an Under-21 game?

A. *Yes, I was selected to play against Belgium and I played the full 90 minutes. We won 1-0 with George McCluskey scoring the only goal. The team included Gordon Strachan, Roy Aitken and Alan Brazil as I recall.*

Q. Any chance of a photograph of you wearing the Scotland cap?
A. *Sorry John, no.*

Q. Any chance of a picture of you with your Player of the Year award?
A. *Again sorry, no! I sold it some years ago along with my Player of the Year trophy, my promotion medal and, in fact, all my memorabilia to a lifelong Morton fan who is a multimillionaire.*

I don't need cups, trophies and medals - I have my memories.

Q. I understand, and maybe you could explain. Even though, as we are led to believe, you had disagreements with Jock Stein, you were offered a four-year contract with Celtic, which would have taken you to 1980, but you declined. Why?
A. *I was young, ambitious and, I suppose, arrogant.*

Q. We know that you could have stayed at Celtic for four more years and it is thought that Liverpool made an offer for you too, as did Manchester City. If you compare the honours that those clubs won during the years you were at Morton, with hindsight would you change anything?
A. *No, my only regret is not winning anything at Morton.*

Q. But you won the First Division Championship and the Player of the Year award whilst playing for Morton and also the Adidas Silver Boot, second only to Paolo Rossi?
A. *Yes! But I can't help thinking that if we had been full-time we could have competed on an equal playing field. Other clubs like Celtic, Rangers, Aberdeen and Dundee all had full-time players. Our lads worked in the shipyards for 40 hours, trained twice a week and I worked in the meat market. It*

wasn't the bed of roses the players have today. If Morton players had been full-time I believe we would have won the Premier League title and played in Europe.

I read somewhere about a bloke who wrote into the newspapers about me being second to Paolo Rossi. I flew to Brussels with Hal Stewart after I was leading in the Golden Boot award but was pipped on the line by Rossi. When he arrived Adidas offered Rossi £25,000 a year to endorse their boots. I wore them because I liked them. When they gave me the Silver Boot they offered me £500. I said 'no thank you' and Hal and I flew back. I went to work the next day in the meat market. Later I signed a deal with Puma for £1,000. A parcel from them would appear every week with tracksuits and other clothing.

Q. You were offloaded to Morton and made your debut on 28th October 1976 at Cappielow Park vs Clydebank. What can you recall about that game?
A. *It was a 0-0 draw so, despite what you might have heard, I did not score on my debut for Morton.*

Q. Benny Rooney and his assistant Mike Jackson were at Morton during the glory years. Where are they now? Do you see them?
A. *Yes I see them both, usually at charity dinners or sportsmen's functions. I think Benny is 'mine host' at the Queen's Park Café in Glasgow. Well, that's what I heard.*

Q. You played several times against Celtic after your move and scored against The Hoops. How did you feel at the time?
A. *When you sign for a new club you don't forget the time spent at your previous club, but my time at Morton was special. I have no regrets, apart from not winning the Premier title for the wonderful fans at Cappielow.*

Q. In 1979 you astounded everybody by being voted Scottish Football Writers' Player of the Year. At the time did you really appreciate the significance of the honour?

A. *Oh yes. Photographs in the papers, a silver salver - special moments.*

Q. Also in 1979, on 1st December Morton played Aberdeen in the semi-final of the Bell's League Cup at Hampden Park. Willie Miller OBE and Scotland Hall of Fame inductee captained The Dons. What are your recollections of the big day?

A. *We lost 2-1. I scored but Archibald scored and the rest, as they say, is history.*

Q. Willie Miller and several other players who received the Footballer of the Year award, including John Grieg and Danny McGrain, were later inducted into the Scotland Hall of Fame. Are you surprised that after 25 years you are still waiting to be inducted?

A. *I thought you had to have 50 caps.*

Q. I have a programme from Celtic dated 11th August 1979 in which the writer says some very gracious things about Morton and yourself. Although Morton lost 3-2, what are your recollections of your return to Parkhead, as it was in those days?

A. *There were things that happened when I was at Celtic that I can't tell you about today. But I will tell all at some point in the future, and my revelations will rock the football world and Celtic to the core.*

Later I was chief scout for Celtic and, of course, I had some good times. I am actually credited with bringing Mark Viduka to the club from Zagreb and other players.

Oh, Celtic are a great club, but some of the things that went on there - well, they wouldn't be allowed to happen today, and nor should they.

Q. Would you like to expand on that statement?

A. *No, not at this time, but I will some day.*

Q. I read somewhere that you are perhaps the best home-grown player never to have pulled on a jersey for Scotland. I think you are an honest enough guy to answer this question. Could you have made the grade as a Scotland international if you had been given the chance by Jock Stein?

A. *There was a lot of talk about my forming an international partnership with Kenny Dalglish.*

Q. How do you think that would have developed?

A. *It could have been great. Kenny could have taught me a great deal about football. I could have taught him a thing or two about humility.*

Q. Long before the Bosman ruling, I understand that several English clubs did approach Morton to buy you, but these overtures were allegedly blocked by Hal Stewart. Were you ever made aware of any offers from English clubs?

A. *No! But I heard about them years later. Liverpool made a bid, which was rejected. I was invited for trials at Newcastle United and trained with them for two weeks, and then they signed Mark McGhee. Celtic even tried to re-sign me. Jack Charlton at Sheffield Wednesday, I heard, offered somewhere around £300,000 and Brighton, who were in the top flight, also bid more than £400,000 I was told years later. There was also interest from Nottingham Forest and Leeds.*

Q. Hal Stewart is quoted as saying he thought he could get £1 million for you. Do you think you were worth that figure?

A. *Morton sold Neil Orr, a defender, to West Ham for £440,000 and Joe McLaughlin to Chelsea for £95,000, so I think Hal thought that as a proven goalscorer I had to be worth a million. It did me no favours, as this was before Andy Gray became a million pound man. My price tag - although I was never told what it was - frightened off the so-called big clubs.*

Q. Liverpool allegedly made an offer that, according to some sources, was £5,000 short of what Morton wanted. Would you have relished going to Liverpool and perhaps teaming up with Kenny Dalglish?

A. *Yes, as I said, I could have learned a lot from Kenny on the football side.*

Q. Graham Taylor from Watford also had you watched before he became the national coach for England. Would you have joined Watford?

A. *I have the utmost respect for Graham Taylor and later in my life I worked with him at Aston Villa. Have a look at Graham's autobiography - he has his views on my career.*

Q. Back to Morton. Is it true that Hal once took you to a health farm to lose weight?

A. *Yes, he checked me into Stobbo Castle where I met the owner, Stephen Wynyard. Lulu and Joan Collins were also there during my stay, and across the hall were four stewardesses from a Saudi airline and a Saudi princess.*

Q. And did you lose weight?

A. *Yes, I lost a stone and a half.*

"Why am I not surprised when you were in that company?" I quipped.

Q. Mike Jackson, Benny Rooney's assistant, says Morton would not have stayed in the SPL for so long had it not been for you. Do you agree?

A. *It was a team effort. There were other lads who made different contributions. But, above everything else, Morton Football Club was a 'team'.*

Q. Fans tell me you scored against Alan Rough, the Scottish international goalkeeper, for fun. Is that true?

A. *Oh, for 23 years on the Saturday lunchtime sports*

programme they would open the show with me scoring past Roughie. Once I was in the 'blue room' [the hospitality suite] *at the TV studio doing a live show. The phone rang and the receptionist answered. "It's for you Andy," she said. It was Roughie asking if I could ask the BBC to sell him the tape of the goal. He was totally cheesed off with being made to look a complete idiot each week. I have cleaned up the conversation for younger readers! I don't know whether he ever got the tape.*

Q. Maybe the BBC will show it again?
A. *Maybe, but not if Roughie has his way. I think he has bought the rights to the recording to stop it being shown.*

Q. You once scored a goal from the halfway line, long before the much publicised effort from David Beckham. Can you remember the incident?
A. *Yes I can, but there seems to be some confusion. Some people say it was Jim Leighton in goal. Although I did score past the goalie with ease, it wasn't Jim. Others say it was a guy called Hamish McAlpine at Dundee United, but my recollection is that it was Peter Bonetti, who had signed for Dundee United as an emergency replacement for an injured keeper. Peter was setting out his stall to be a postman on the Isle of Mull. But on this occasion it was Andy Ritchie who made a first-class delivery.*

Q. You have always had a good relationship with the press, presumably because over the years you gave them so much to write about. How do you get on with Chick Young, the broadcaster with the BBC? He describes you as the epitome of the Scottish footballer - "fat, lazy bastard but with great ball skill"?
A. *Chick Young always had something caustic to say about most people.*

Q. Have you ever played for Young's charity soccer team,

Dukla Pumpherston, whom he describes as a drinking team with a football problem?

A. *Well, I was a founder member of Dukla with actor Tony Roper, who was a pal of Rab C. Nesbitt. But Chick may not recall that, or maybe old age has taken over. I have been a member of Dukla Pump for some 25 years.*

Q. Would you liken Chick Young to Alex Young or, say, Davie Cooper?

A. *More like Jimmy Young and Tommy Cooper!* laughed Andy.

Q. Having listened to the fans in the Spinnaker Hotel and the Albert Hotel in Gourock and eavesdropped on conversations at Cappielow Park, I don't think even now you ever appreciated the high regard in which you were held. Don't you realise the fans worshipped you?

A. *Well, I did and I didn't. But as long as I was there and I made them happy - well, I was happy too. I meet them occasionally and have attended a few charity functions at the Spinnaker Hotel. The boss, Stewart, well he's more like a friend. Great bloke!*

Q. You have been described as the greatest ever Scottish entertainer on the football field. How does that make you feel now?

A. Andy just smiled. *Look John, at times I am accused of being flippant but the bottom line is I enjoyed playing football. I liked scoring goals. I liked entertaining the fans. They were everything to me.*

Q. Jim McLean, the Dundee boss at the time, described one of your goals as one of the greatest he had ever seen, but you just brushed off his praise. Why?

A. *Sometimes people are pressured into making a comment by the press. You have to look at comments rather than take them out of context. But Jim McLean knew a good goal when he saw one.*

Q. *Telegraph* reporter Roger Graham, now Sports Editor, expressed surprise when you tackled an opponent before scoring one goal. So you didn't like tackling?

A. *Is Roger still around? What he knows about football is contained in the centre of a doughnut. [One of Andy's little jokes. Roger has a wealth of knowledge about the beautiful game.] He was only a young, snotty-nosed reporter back then, but again I am pleased he has risen through the journalistic ranks. He deserves his success. I believed that defenders tackled forwards not vice versa. Roger is entitled to his opinion. I have mine. That's the beauty of football. We can argue, agree to disagree, but at the end of the day there's no need to fall out with anybody.*

Q. What about heading the ball, something that I know worried your mum?

A. *I didn't need to head the ball. I was well over 6 feet and some of my contemporaries were vertically challenged. They still are. Gordon Strachan, for example, is 5 foot 6 inches tall and I was over 6 foot 1 - those seven inches are important. Anybody who tells you size doesn't matter is telling porkies.*

Q. And you didn't like training according to some people?

A. *Again, you have to look at the overall picture. I was getting up at 6 a.m. to work in the meat market in Glasgow. We were all part-timers at Morton. I put in a full shift humping meat about, and when I clocked off I had to travel two hours to the training session, train with the lads and then travel two hours back home. It was no picnic and, yes, I hated training.*

Q. So what made you so special?

A. *I don't think I am special. I never said I was. I think that was Jose Mourinho. I was in the right place at the right time. I scored goals and entertained people. Simple as that. Score goals and keep the fans happy and entertained.*

Q. What was your best goal ever? Pundits say the goal you

scored in the 1-0 fourth round win over Aberdeen on Valentine's Day 1981. Hardly a massacre, but do you think it was the best?
A. *No!*

Q. Then which one?
A. *Take your pick, John, there's 133 to choose from* he laughed.

Q. When you finally left Morton for Motherwell, what was your transfer fee?
A. *I seem to recall the fee was £35,000 ... or was it £50,000? I can't remember.*

Q. What were your wages at Morton?
A. *We were all part-timers, as I mentioned - on £50 a week.*

Q. And at Motherwell?
A. *Again, I don't recall. It was never about money. I just wanted to play football.*

Q. Did you know that Joe McLaughlin was sold to Chelsea from Morton at about the same time for £95,000?
A. *Yes, I heard that.*

Q. Is it realistic that you could have commanded such a fee with a move south of the border?
A. *You are only worth what people are prepared to pay is the simple answer.*

Q. Neil Orr went to West Ham United and played for the Hammers 146 times. How much did they pay Morton?
A. *I heard it was £440,000, but you would need to check that with Neil.*

Q. After your spell as player/manager with Albion Rovers, did you ever dream of managing Morton?

A. *Oh, I didn't only dream about becoming manager of Morton, I actually applied for the manager's job before Jim McInally was installed. Not only did I not get the job, my application didn't even warrant an acknowledgement.*

Q. When you were at Albion Rovers, you resurrected the career of another player who you had seen at Morton. Who was that?
A. *Bernie Slaven. I told Bernie if he came and did a similar job for me at Rovers to the one I had done at Morton, it would put him in line for a move to a bigger club.*

Q. And did it?
A. *After Bernie was awarded the Golden Boot for his season at Albion Rovers from the Daily Record and then wrote to every First and Second Division club in England, he got his dream move. Bernie was sold to Middlesbrough for £25,000, where he too became a legend.*

Q. In the many words written about you it says you retired at just 27 and took a job outside football - doing what?
A. *I went to London and took a Business Management course as a mature student at North London Polytechnic. When I graduated I was appointed assistant manager at the Barbican Centre in London EC1. I took part-time jobs to put myself through college, including one as a car park attendant.*

Q. How long was it before you missed the beautiful game?
A. *I had a good job, good money and the kids got a good education in London, but every day I missed football. My wife had a good job as an optician and we had a good lifestyle. But I suppose there is a bit of the homing pigeon in all of us and you can smell the heather on a true Scotsman. I was always bound to come home.*

I came home to see my mum and met a lad I knew, Jimmy Dempsey. Jimmy was at Hamilton at the time. He offered me the assistant manager's job and I returned north with the family.

John Wilson, the former chairman and a lifelong Morton supporter, told me he was thinking of buying Morton after he retired from his ship-dredging business. I thought at first he might be spinning a yarn but true to his word he bought the club and approached me to return to Cappielow.

Q. What happened next?
A. *I was interviewed by Douglas Rae at Buchanan Toffees and I signed for Morton and came down to meet Allan McGraw.*

Alan knew nothing about the deal until he was informed after a board meeting. He told me that if he'd wanted an assistant he would have appointed Jackie McNamara snr not me.

He said at the time, "You are a threat to me. If I lose three games in a row the crowd will be shouting for you."

John Wilson kept me at Morton for six months.

I did very little, but I didn't want to make the facts public at the time because I respected both Allan and Mr Wilson. The chairman continued to pay me and I had a company car, but I had nothing to do.

I wanted to work at Morton, but Allan McGraw did a terrific job. He was honest with me and I respect him for that. I see him at dinners and socials and I hold him in the highest regard.

Q. Are you a shareholder at Morton?
A. *No.*

Q. Do you do the Morton lotto every week?
A. *Oh, I have done it on the odd occasion.*

At this point we collected a lottery form from the Spinnaker Hotel and chose our numbers for the weekend using a combination of Andy's date of birth, the number of goals he scored and the temperature at the time. Needless to say, we didn't win the jackpot!

Q. When you left Morton, as realistically there wasn't a job for you to do, what happened then?

A. *I went to work for a chemical company in Glasgow to help out another old friend. I stayed there for four years and I was brilliant at selling. I could sell the proverbial ice cream to Eskimos. In the end my pal sold out to one of the largest competitors in Scotland and he retired aged just 53. He is still retired.*

Q. What did you do then?

A. *Tommy Burns asked me if I would help him at Celtic and assume responsibility for running the youth team.*

Q. How did it feel going back to Celtic after all those years?

A. *Oh, it was great. Everybody was okay.*

Q. Then what?

A. *Then I had a spell as assistant manager at St Mirren under Jimmy Bone. I don't have any coaching badges, but two lads at the club were qualified - Campbell Money, who was at Ayr United, and Kenny McDowall, who had been at Rangers.*

They refused to stand near me in the dugout, as the St Mirren fans hated me because of my association with Morton.

The dugout at Love Street was a contradiction in terms, as there was certainly no love lost between me and the Saints fans. When things were going wrong, the Saints fans hurled abuse at me, calling me a 'soap dodging badger'.

I didn't ask what was meant by that 'term of endearment'!

Q. I am off to see Hamilton Academicals play Morton at the weekend and you are going to see Dundee vs Rangers in your capacity as an SPL delegate. Want to swap games?

A. *I would love to go to the Morton game, but my son is moving into a new house this week. Going to Dundee is my bread and butter these days. I really do enjoy being involved - involved in football, meeting football people, talking football. Well, football was and still is an important part of my life.*

Q. Where do you expect Morton to finish this season?
A. *They should do well. The manager seems to be getting them to play and I hope they consolidate their position in the League. But it will take some effort to catch Hamilton, even at this stage of the season.*

Q. Is it possible that Morton can do a Gretna and get back into the SPL at sometime in the near future?
A. *Morton have been in the SPL. We lived the dream, beating Rangers, Celtic and Aberdeen without the Gretna money. Morton is a club with history and a loyal fan base, and money can't buy that.*

Q. You were once described as a chief scout at Celtic. Can you spot talent? Have you seen any good young players that we should look out for?
A. *Oh, I can spot talent, of that there is no doubt. Ask John Gregory, the former Villa boss, Graham Taylor and the people at Celtic. I know talent when I see it. I can't tell you any young players' names - it wouldn't be fair.*

Q. What does your role as an SPL delegate entail?
A. *Broadly speaking, I am an observer. I go to games and observe many aspects of the game - the reaction of the crowd, the managers, the referee - and send in a report to the SFA.*

My final two questions were about two subjects that Scottish fans are debating at the moment.

Q. What impact has the influx of foreign players had on the Scottish game and is this to the benefit or detriment of the national side?
A. *In the first instance they improved the quality of play. We brought people like Henrik Larsen to the club and Rangers*

bought Brian Ladrupp, but not every foreign player settles. In so far as the national side is concerned, it is my belief that Scotland was held back for eight or nine years, but now we are reaping the benefits.

Q. There has been a growing campaign asking for modern technology to be used, to make action replays available for instance, as is the case in rugby league and cricket. How do you think we should use modern technology, if at all?

A. *As far as modern technology is concerned, I say if it's there use it. It's going to happen. Andy Gray of Sky TV is a wise, wise man and he said more than ten years ago that we should embrace modern technology. How very right he was.*

Having concluded my interview questions, I spent the next four hours talking to Andy about football, Morton and so many other matters associated with the beautiful game.

At one point we talked about Mr Jimmy McCartney, an old director at Morton whom I'd read had suddenly died during Andy's playing years at Morton. An acknowledgement of his death was printed in a Celtic programme I own.

Andy said he regarded Mr McCartney as a real gentleman, and then went on to tell me about a game in 1977 at Broomfield Street versus Airdrie.

Airdrie scored first and at half-time Morton were trailing behind. However, after a rousing half-time talk from Benny Rooney, The Ton came back and Ritchie scored two goals. The dressing room after the game was bubbly and happy. It was a great fightback.

Once they had showered, Andy, Jimmy Goldthorpe and Jim Holmes decided they would go for a pint on the way home. Andy said, "I had about three quid on me, so we stopped at a village called Whifflet."

To his surprise, when he came to pay for his drink he found a bundle of notes in his pocket. He had no idea where they had come from, but said nothing to his teammates.

Andy takes up the story:

"The next day when we trained I went to see the manager and explained what I had found. He said he would make some enquiries. Later it transpired that Jimmy McCartney was so pleased with our fightback and my contribution that he had slipped £100 into my pocket whilst we were in the showers.

"A few days later I passed him in the corridor at the club and thanked him. His response was that I deserved it because my goals had given him so much pleasure.

"Another time he took me horse racing at Carlisle and another time we called into the stables of Sir Gordon Richards, where I met champion jockey Ron Barry. Mr McCartney was a millionaire and horse racing was his hobby.

"It wasn't the last time I met personalities from the world of racing. Tote bookmakers asked me if I would share the honour in opening their new shops in Greenock and Gourock - with triple Grand National winner Red Rum."

Finally I asked Andy about the problems I had heard about on the terraces regarding his relationship with Douglas Rae. I had been told by fans that Mr Rae had invested almost £2 million in the Morton club and was disappointed that he never received the recognition he felt he deserved. It was also rumoured that, when Mr Rae discovered that he wasn't even mentioned in one book about the club, he refused to allow the book to be sold in the club's shop. Of course it has been almost impossible to validate these rumours. There is always somebody wanting to add two and two together to make five.

"Look, John, I don't have a problem with Douglas Rae. He has spent millions and if he expected thanks or adulation from the fans and that wasn't forthcoming it has nothing to do with me.

"I received the hero worship, praise, adulation, whatever you want to call it, because I scored goals and entertained the fans at Cappielow. I didn't need to buy that.

"The owner of a football club never really owns a club. Morton Football Club is an institution. Any owner, past or present, is just the 'custodian' for the time he has his/her money invested in the club.

139

"Morton Football Club is not just those buildings at Cappielow Park or the current group of players or the staff. Morton Football Club has 125 years of history and a loyal fan base.

"In truth, Morton Football Club belongs to the people."

Jimmy Reid would have been proud to hear Andy say that.

As our meeting drew to a close and my fingers ached from writing, we moved on to family matters.

"My family is my hobby, John. I love my dear old mum and I hope she lives to be 120. I love my two sons and my granddaughter, my little princess - yes, I am a grandfather. I also have a mongrel dog who lives most of the time at my mum's. The dog is called Cara."

You get the real feeling that Andy Ritchie is truly a family man. His 'extended family' also includes those friends he has made in the beautiful game. These days he adopts the persona of a 'subject' rather than a 'king'.

We then talked about food. Andy loves Italian food and fresh fish, which may account for his slimline figure today. That wasn't the case when he was playing, with his heavyweight boxing frame that today would have attracted chants of "You fat bastard" from rival fans.. He has only the occasional pint of lager, despite what you might have read, and thoroughly enjoys a glass of red wine.

When Andy does find himself in front of the television, this big brute of a footballer enjoys programmes about animals, football of course, and most programmes shown in English as he does spend some time abroad, which may increase if a current job opportunity comes to fruition - in football of course.

These days he drives a four-year-old Vauxhall Vectra - a little different from when he had four cars a year from one of Morton's sponsors, Alexander Motors, the local Ford dealer. The best car he ever had was a BMW McLaren, but then, as Andy says, a car is just a vehicle to get you from A to B.

Just as we were about to leave the Spinnaker Hotel we bumped into Jim Sinclair, a local photographer, whom I had contacted because I knew he and Andy once clashed - in a verbal sense, not a physical one. It was apparently during a game on a blistering run (now I knew somebody was embroidering a little here, because Andy never had a blistering run in him) and Jim recalled the incident when Andy came crashing down on him. Jim was a photographer working for the *Greenock Telegraph* at the time and the fans at the game gave Jim a lashing because they feared his stool and camera box had caused injury to Andy.

Never one to miss an opportunity, I snapped Andy and Jim together again after more than 25 years, this time in a more sedate setting. My photograph was not up to Jim's standards. Jim now works for the police as a crime scene investigator, but he still retains fond memories of games at Cappielow Park.

It took quite a while to walk from our dinner table in the hotel, as each step of the way people wanted to stop and talk to the gentle giant. He signed programmes and a hastily produced Morton shirt - do you Morton fans always carry one in case you bump into a player? Nothing was too much trouble for the big guy, who was only too happy to chat.

As Andy was finally about to leave, he dropped a bombshell.

He suggested that if I really wanted to pen a best-seller we should meet again. He would then be prepared to discuss two issues that would rock the very foundations of football: the old chestnut of bungs in relation to the transfer of players from one club to another; the payments people received; the clubs, players and money involved.

He then went on to mention an infinitely more serious subject - a paedophile ring at a Premiership club.

Rock the foundations of football? It certainly rocked mine.

I cautioned Andy that if we proceeded with a second book as he was suggesting, he should think carefully. He wouldn't only have to talk to an ageing Sports Editor but more than likely 'the Old Bill'.

Andy disappeared into the cold night air as the mist was drifting in across the River Clyde. He arrived in Gourock at 12.30 p.m. and finally made his way back to Glasgow just before 8 p.m.

Things were revealed in the interview with Andy that I checked and double-checked with him, as a great deal of the information has never been made known in the public domain. I am sure I will have missed something from that first day I spent with him, but there will be others.

It was indeed a great pleasure to have this rare opportunity of an exclusive interview with one of Scotland's and Greenock Morton's legends - 'the King of Cappielow', Andy Ritchie.

I returned to the Spinnaker for a 'wee dram'. It had been an eventful day and I was shattered.

Whatever the future holds for Andy Ritchie remains to be seen, but what is apparent is that fans when they meet him today still hold him in as high regard as when he truly was 'The King of Cappielow'.

Postscript

In my exclusive interview with Andy Ritchie, he revealed that it was his intention to share with me, for our next book together, details on two controversial subjects that would rock the very foundations of the football world.

Firstly, Andy agreed to talk exclusively to me about legal/illegal payments that have changed hands in connection with the transfer of players, naming the players, the clubs and the amounts of money involved.

Secondly, Andy wished to share the secret that he had kept locked away for more than 30 years, and I cautioned Andy when he told me its content, as making public the information he has relating to sexual abuse of young players at a Premiership club would mean he would be subjected to interviews by the police rather than 'gentle' journalists such as myself.

Did Andy realise the far-reaching implications of his planned revelations?

A few months later, having reflected on his parting shot on that October evening, Andy Ritchie asked me to delete the draft final chapter on sexual abuse and bungs, and I have adhered to Andy's request and removed the chapter.

My research in the interim period had revealed the circumstances of some sexual abuse, the court dates and the sentences of the court. It also suggested other individuals who might have been implicated. This information is a matter of public record and already in the hands of the police.

Developments in the south of England, with the arrest of a well-known manager, an agent and the owner of a football club, confirmed to me that this was an inappropriate time to muddy the waters in that current investigation.

As Andy said, "It could be a best-seller," but on another day. I would like readers to remember my book for the right reasons -

Andy Ritchie's great days at Morton Football Club and the impact he made on football at Greenock - rather than some of the more unsavoury aspects of the beautiful game.

This is my tribute to Andy Ritchie - the uncrowned 'King of Cappielow'.

www.apexpublishing.co.uk